Reschofsky

Secrets of the Sea

A Golden Hands book

Marshall Cavendish, London

Pictures supplied by

Front cover:
Four-eyed butterfly fish (Bruce Coleman)

Back cover:
Sea-horse (Grossa-Jacana)
Acanthurus (Visage-Jacana)

Atlas-Photo
Bertot 9
Mignard 60 below
Rives 41 top
Schultz 44 top
Sillner 19
Six 59
Barthelemy 15
Jacana
Bassot 65
Carre 38
Chaumeton 27, 34
Grossa 61
Kerneis 44 below
Klemm 68
Noailles 14 top, 14 below
Ousoff 72
Schraml 77
Sundance 53 top, 53 below
Viellard 58
Visage 37, 43, 60 middle left, 60 middle right, 67
Holmes-Lebel 71, 74, 75
Meusy 24, 30, 45, 50
Rapho
Lecuziat 31
Myers 10
De Sazo 18
Thompson 49
Zuber 69
Starosta 32, 41 below, 60 top

Edited by Humphrey Evans

Translated by Richard Marsden

Published by Marshall Cavendish Publications Limited,
58 Old Compton Street, London W1V.

© Marshall Cavendish Publications Limited 1974

© Fernand Nathan, Paris 1972

This volume first printed 1974

ISBN 0 85685 079 9

Printed by Colour Reproductions Limited, Billericay, Essex
and bound by The Wigmore Bindery, Poole, Dorset.

This volume not to be sold in the USA, Canada and the
Philippines.

ABOUT THIS BOOK

The sea has its secrets—and you will share them when you read this book. There are literally dozens of those intriguing questions you've always wanted to know the answers to—and dozens of answers that take you right into the underwater world.

What makes waves?
Is a big crab older than a small one?
Can flying-fish really fly?
How is a baby dolphin born?

The scientifically-accurate text gives the answers in easily-readable sections that are just right for the enquiring mind of a young person —or an adult browsing out of interest or looking up the answers to a child's questions.

Whatever you want to know about the underwater world you can find it in *Secrets of the Sea*. And as you turn the pages you'll find new questions to ask—and the answers. You'll enjoy taking a closer look at life in the sea with *Secrets of the Sea*.

CONTENTS

SEA AND SHORE

What makes waves?

The main cause of waves **is the wind.** If there is a wind storm over one area of the ocean, the waves can break onto beaches thousands of miles away. Of course, they are a lot smaller than they are at the heart of the storm. By studying the rhythm of waves, meteorologists get information on the winds

A huge wave nears the end of its journey.

that caused them.

But the wind is not the only 'wave-maker', because sea-water varies in temperature and in the amount of salt it contains. This means that there are masses of water which, in effect, are independent of each other. These masses with different temperatures and salinities (the amount of salt) do not mix together, but slide against one another. When one mass is sliding over the top of another mass, this can cause underwater waves, which are commonly known as ground swell.

While waves produced by the wind can move along at a rate of more than **60 miles an hour** (100 km. an hour), underwater waves never reach more than **two and a half miles an hour.** On the other hand, they can be three times as high.

How high can waves be?

The height of a wave is the vertical distance between a trough and a crest. It is extremely difficult to measure the height of a wave. When a boat is caught in a storm the people on board tend to say that the waves were, for example, as high as a **ten-storey building.** It is now known that waves can reach a height of **65 feet** (20m.).

What causes the tides?

All liquid matter on the earth is attracted by the moon and the sun. Although the moon is far smaller, its pulling power is greater than the sun's since it is much nearer the earth. Each time the moon is above an ocean the water is attracted by it and swells, drawing away from the coast-line. This happens about twice a day, and since the moon goes round the earth once every 28 days the time of the tides varies from day to day.

Where does sand come from?

The beautiful shining grains of sand that you see on golden beaches are not made by the sea, but are sent back to the land by it. The sand often comes from a long way away. At the start, sand is taken from rocks by the rain or the rivers, and brought down to the sea. It needed the steady, endless beating of the water to slowly file down the pieces of rock and gravel into fine grains of sand. The sand you see on the beach is composed of tiny **crystals of silica** and minute **particles of mica.**

Why is the sea salty?

For millions and millions of years, rivers have deposited in the sea fragments of rock that they have gathered on their journey. Some of these rocks contain salt, and this salt has gradually accumulated in the sea. At the bottom of the oceans, there are also thick layers of salt. This is because there is so much salt in the seas that the water cannot dissolve any more.

Why are icebergs so dangerous?

Are there mountains under the sea?

In the middle of the Atlantic a wide fissure cuts through the earth's crust. The edges of this crack are moving apart at the rate of 1 inch (2 centimetres) every year.

In the polar regions there are large glaciers which flow into the sea like enormous rivers of ice. The huge masses of fresh water, in the form of ice, that are set loose in this way break up and become in effect drifting islands which constitute a great shipping hazard. Icebergs, as they are called, are four-fifths submerged, and so hide the formidable spurs of their jagged edges beneath the water. It is

an unfortunate ship that collides with one! A great deal of care is taken by sailors when navigating through areas where they are likely to encounter an iceberg.

How far do icebergs travel?

Some icebergs can drift a long way away from the Poles, and even reach tropical waters. When this happens, they have to be blown up to avoid shipping disasters in regions where the crew may well not be looking out for such hazards.

Under the sea, the continental shelf that is along the edge of the continents has a similar relief to the one seen above the water. There are deep valleys, hollowed out by rivers long ago, and mountain chains with peaks that sometimes **rise above the water** to form islands like the Azores.

There are also movements of the earth's crust below the water just as there are above it. The underwater earthquakes and volcanoes that these movements cause bear witness to this.

Folds can appear at the bottom of the ocean basin. It has been discovered that the Atlantic Ocean is crossed by a **mountain chain** as impressive as those on land, with jagged peaks and deep valleys. Mauna Loa and Kilauea in the Hawaiian islands are both the summits of volcanoes several thousand feet high. So you can imagine the quantities of smaller volcanoes that are still hidden under the sea.

SOUTH AMERICA

AFRICA

ATLANTIC OCEAN   Fissure

Viscous layer where vortices occur

Why are continents said to float or 'drift'?

First of all, there is no question of them floating on the water—it is not quite as simple as that. In fact, the whole of the earth's crust is formed around a thick layer of molten rocks, like the skin on milk which is about to boil. But this **'earth skin'** varies in thickness. The continents are the thickest parts of it, and geologists think that they float like rafts on a thick layer of matter that is continually melted by the heat coming from the centre of the earth. Since the earth is turning, these rafts move towards, or away from, each other. This is what is known as **continental drift.**

Since the discovery of the Atlantic mountain chain it has also been discovered that a **great ditch** runs across the chain. It is about a mile deep and its edges are moving apart at a rate of **three-quarters of an inch every year.** Over a period of one hundred years, America moves 75 inches away from Europe. And what is a century to the Earth with its millions of years behind it? It is relatively not more than six or seven seconds of a human life . . .

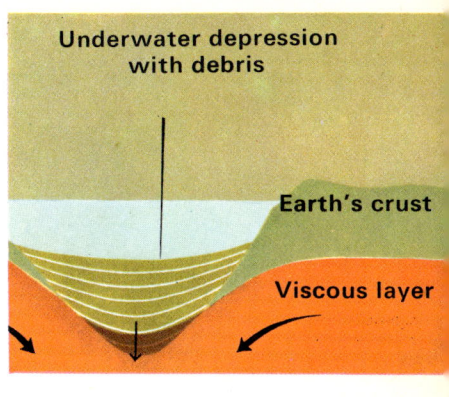

Underwater depression with debris

Earth's crust

Viscous layer

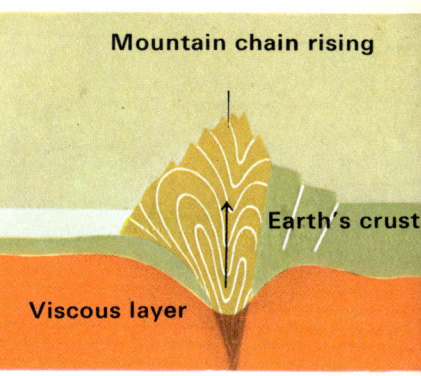

Mountain chain rising

Earth's crust

Viscous layer

The sediment caught between the hard layers of the earth's crust fold and rise up.

Viscous layer

Earth's crust

NORTH AMERICA

EUROPE

ASIA

AFRICA

AUSTRALIA

SOUTH AMERICA

ANTARCTIC

In dark-brown, the earth's crust; in orange, the viscous layer; in the centre, in maroon, the core.

The trilobite is the oldest fossilized type of shell-fish.

Why are shells found on cliff-tops and even on mountainsides?

We need to make one simple deduction: shell-fish do not live on land, so where they are found is where the sea must once have been . . . It is actually not too long ago that this simple reasoning was first made.

Bernard Palissy, a sixteenth-century French potter, was one of the first to think of this explanation. He used a lot of animals as models, and realized that the shells he found in the ground were the **remains** of ancient marine animals.

Most of the ground over which we move has, at one time or another, been covered by the sea. These areas were then lifted up and folded, and then formed plateaux or mountains. The remains of marine animals were preserved in these masses of earth for millions of years. They became almost like stone in the process, and these are what we now call **fossils.**

These ammonites, cephalopods of the Secondary Period, looked very much like nautiluses. Each was like a small octopus enclosed in a shell.

Cliffs like these contain huge quantities of fossils.

A refinery beside a lagoon: today's oil is refined next to tomorrow's.

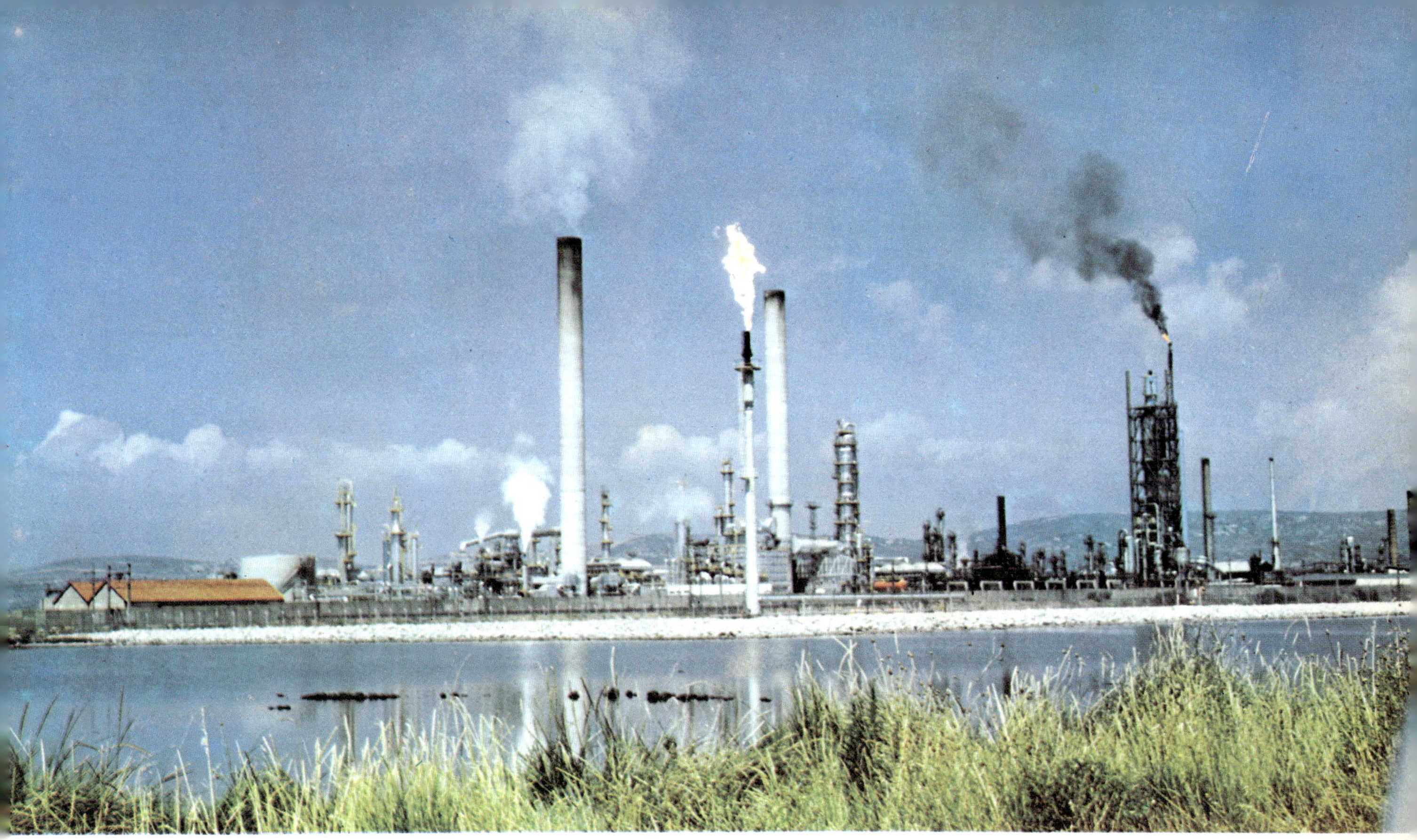

Where does oil come from?

Some foul-smelling coastal lagoons are full of brackish, stagnant water swarming with dying **minute animals.** Fortunately they are gradually filled in by sand, and so the smell eventually disappears. This process of decay is the first stage in the formation of oil.

When prospectors drill a hole in search of oil, they are looking for the lagoon where animals and plants decomposed millions of years before. And since they sometimes have to go deeper than **12,000 feet** to find this precious liquid, the idea of how long it took for these layers of rock to accumulate is staggering.

Animals and algae that have decayed slowly in the slime under layers of clay and sand are what have gone to make up oil.

Engineers fitting a new length to a drill boring into the earth's crust. Nowadays, drilling can go to a depth of more than 12,000 feet.

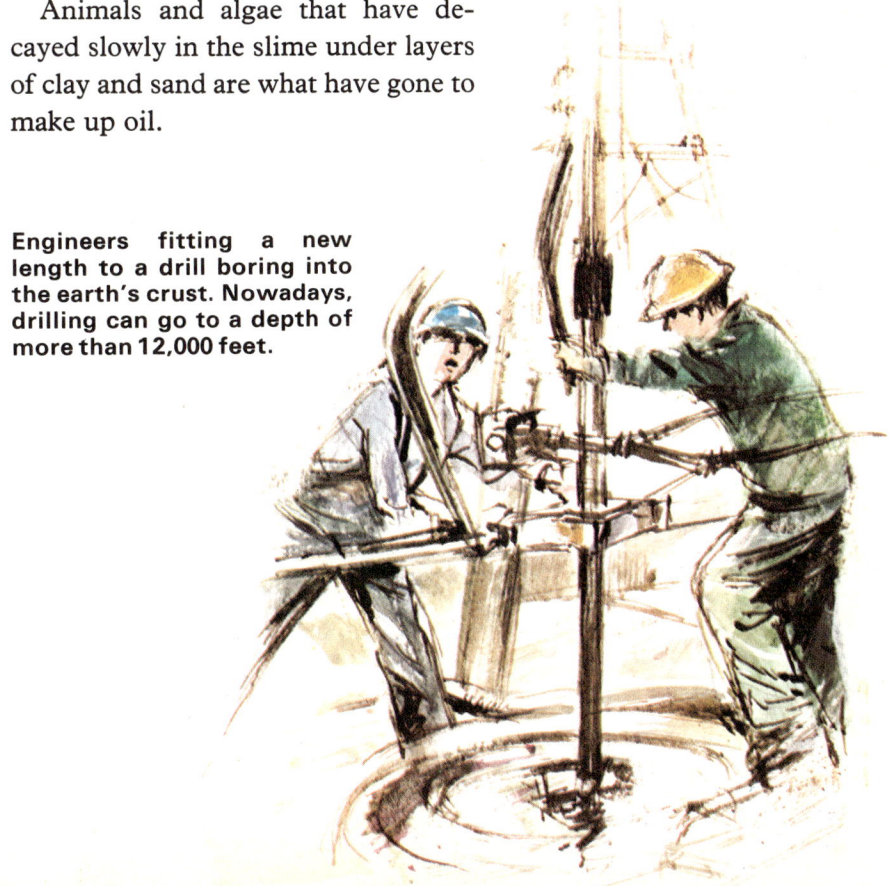

What is plankton?

Plankton may be the food of the future. There has been a great deal of speculation about plankton since experiments were carried out that might help ship-wrecked sailors survive. The small inflatable rubber dinghies, that are now a standard part of survival kit for sailors and airmen, contain a small very fine-mesh net to catch plankton. With these nets the occupants can catch enough plankton to prevent them from starving. Plankton might one day rule out hunger in the world.

Plankton is an overall term used to designate everything that drifts along at the mercy of the waves. Algae, jelly-fish, marine microbes, shell-fish and fish—when they cannot fight against the currents—are all examples of plankton life. But the term is most often used to describe the tiny organisms that are found in the sea: for example, alevin, minute shell-fish and microscopic algae. In fact, plankton is everything that makes up the food of a whale, whose **whalebones** prevent it from swallowing anything more than **one and a half inches** long. And since a whale is such an enormous creature, plankton must be really nourishing!

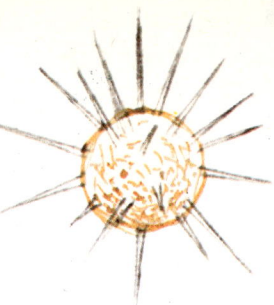

This spiky ball is the siliceous shell of a microscopic single-celled animal.

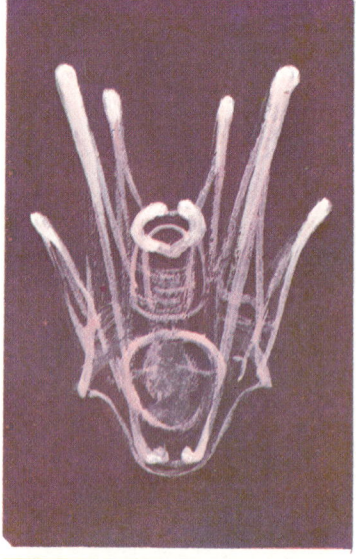

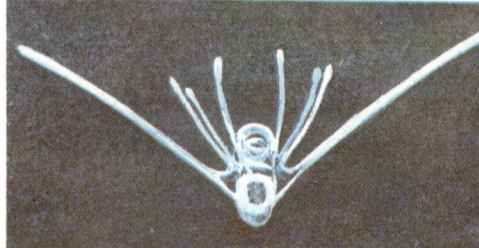

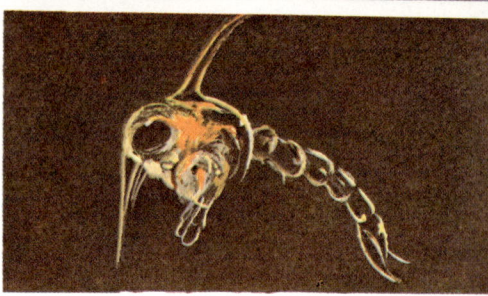

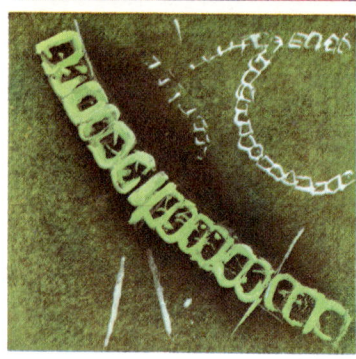

Top left: Star-fish larva. Top right: Sea-urchin larva. Bottom left: String of single-celled green algae. Bottom right: Crab larva—this kind is called a zoea.

When you look at plankton through a microscope you come across some strange shapes. There are small shell-fish with shells like rose-windows and small boxes of silica, decorated like jewel-boxes, with algae inside them. These shells and caskets would provide an infinite variety of lace-work patterns.

Why is the sea sometimes green or red?

Plankton, which floats near the surface of the sea is made up of microscopic algae which are the sea's great treasure, for they constitute the food of the great mass of marine animals. There are great numbers and varieties of them.

When the conditions are right, some species of microscopic algae proliferate until wide stretches of sea take on the colour of their red or green pigment.

The colour of the sea is an indication of how rich it is in vegetable plankton.

Are all algae edible?

Some of them are poisonous, and if there are enormous quantities of them they can actually poison the sea. As a result, large amounts of fish are killed. This happens, for example, with certain red algae which cause the deadly **red tides** that litter the beaches with thousands of dead fish.

Is seaweed the only type of plant that grows in the sea?

Algae are the most widespread plant family to be found in the sea: from microscopic strands to seaweed **dozens of yards** long. There are many varieties of them, but nevertheless they are not the only plants in the sea.

In shallow water there can often be found **whole meadows** of green healthy grass. These plants are in no way inferior to their counterparts on the land, and indeed these flowering plants did originally come from the land. They have followed the same path as the mammals that now live in the sea. They left the sea at the beginning of life's conquest of the submerged areas, and later returned with their evolution into superior, flowering plants completed. Their **pollen** is dispersed by the underwater currents in the same way that the air carries grains of pollen over the land.

But you will never find ferns or mosses in the sea. Apart from the algae, there are only a few flowering grasses and the occasional mushroom.

Large species of seaweed (algae) can only live in shallow water because they need light to survive. They are found in a great variety of colours, which are produced by pigments that use the light to feed the plant with the carbonic gas that is dissolved in the water. There are varieties of green, brown and red seaweed.

A meadow of sea-grass (zostera). This is not a form of algae, but a plant that reproduces itself by flowering. In this respect, it is just like many plants that grow on land.

JELLY·FISH AND CORALS

WORMS AND MOLLUSCS

Why do jelly-fish leave you a sting to remember them by?

A jelly-fish that has been stranded on a beach looks, not surprisingly, like a big lump of jelly. But this jelly is enclosed in a very thin bag which ends in long strands.

The entire surface of a jelly-fish—and particularly its tentacles—bristles with **small harpoons.** At the slightest touch, these harpoons swell up and inject a poison into the offending skin. Small fish are paralysed, and humans feel severe pain. But if an unlucky swimmer has the misfortune to repeat the experience within the next few days, he can be **paralysed** and even **faint.**

It is not possible to become immune to jelly-fish stings. On the contrary, you become more and more sensitive to them. All close relatives of the jelly-fish have the same defence mechanism: the **sea-anemone** and the **polypary,** for example.

Different sorts of stinging jelly-fish. From top to bottom: Aurelia Cotylorhiza, Rhizostoma, Chrysaora. Inset: Polyorchis.

What is coral?

When you look at a piece of coral you would hardly suspect that it is, in fact, the **outside skeleton of an animal.** But that is just what it is!

Colonies of **hydroida**—cousins of the jelly-fish and the sea anemones—have built up these amazing structures. Hydroida are soft, very fragile animals that protect themselves by hiding in limestone boxes, just like the snail hides in its shell. When they wish to eat, only their tentacles (six or eight, depending on the species) emerge and **open out like flowers** on the existing surface of the coral. They are also called polyps or polyparies. These tiny creatures can form huge colonies of varying shapes and colours. Some species have massive skeletons, with furrows all over them like a brain and can weigh **more than a ton.** Some grow out into branches like a deer's antlers; others build reefs.

Where is the largest reef?

The biggest of these reefs is off the coast of Australia. This reef, which is called the Great Barrier Reef, is **500 feet high,** with a surface area of **125,000 square miles.**

Reef corals can only flourish in waters with a temperature of between 77 and 83°F (25 to 29°C). They need a great deal of light, and consequently they are only found around the equator.

How many sorts of coral are there?

There also exist hydroida with a flexible calcareous skeleton. These are the **gorgonia** and are called sea-fans, sea-pens or sea-whips, depending on the form they take.

Corals can be found in many colours —blue, red, yellow, green and others. They often get their colouring from the **minute algae** that have made their way into the individual cells. Coral reefs shelter great quantities and varieties of marine life.

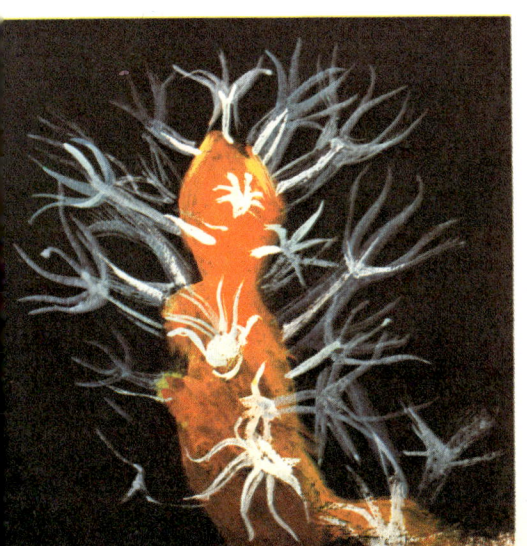

What is an atoll?

An atoll is the result of a **combined effort** between the land and the corals. Coral only grows well in clear water that is well exposed to the sun. This means that at a depth of 200 feet its growth rate is almost nil. And yet it is possible to find coral reefs that go down several hundred feet below the surface.

At these depths there are no more polyps in the calcareous cells—but there must have been at some time. Otherwise the cells would not be there! This is understandable only if we assume that the sea-bed has subsided in these areas.

Atolls can only be found in those parts of the ocean where the sea bottom is of a **volcanic nature.** On the spot where we now see a ring-shaped island, thousands of years ago there stood a volcano rising up out of the sea. Gradually it sank down, taking with it the coral-shoals that had built up on its sides under the water. The subsidence was slow enough for the corals to build new cells and so move higher up.

How high can the coral rise?

Research carried out in the **Eniwetok** atoll near **Bikini,** part of the Marshall islands in the Pacific, has shown that a **5,000 foot** high coral wall was built above the volcanic lava on which it rested. The minute hydroida that build these coral-shoals are the **greatest builders** in the world. They have both time and numbers on their side.

A ring of coconut trees surrounds the calm lagoon.

Are there marine animals with sails?

Above: a flotilla of Velella. Left: the underside of a Velella. Far left: a Portuguese man-of-war, with its long poisonous tentacles. Sometimes these tentacles can become detached and float on the surface. Since they are transparent, an unlucky swimmer can easily be stung by them.

Man is not the only one to have thought of using the wind to move along by means of a sail. With their strange natural sails the velella and the physalia—both cousins of the jellyfish—and the paper nautilus, which is a mollusc, drift at the mercy of the winds. The velella's sail is like a translucent shell; the physalia is propelled along by a large **transparent bell full of air.** As for the paper nautilus, it stays at the very top of its shell and it is a large outgrowth of this shell that actually catches the wind.

A flotilla of velella in shades of pale pink and mauve is a pretty sight. But keep well away from the physalia, because from beneath its bell stretch long strands covered with **poisonous darts.** These are what have given it the nick-name of 'Portuguese man-of-war'.

What are those strange tubes that come out of the sand at low tide?

These funny-looking tubes are very much like lengths of screening for electric wires. At high tide, under the sea, their ends open out into magnificent **purple and pink corollas** which rotate slowly. The moment a shadow passes over these 'flowers' they withdraw immediately into the tube with animal swiftness.

The **spirographis** is a worm; it forms a protective sheath of mucus and sand around itself to prevent it from drying up when the tide goes out. **It captures its minute prey** with the long filaments around its mouth because it is rooted in the sand like a plant and cannot move.

Above: a spirographis unfurls its magnificent corolla. Below: the foot of a spirographis that has let go of the sandy bottom.

There are a great many kinds of marine worms. The most beautiful are those with iridescent byssi, or threads. These threads are sometimes very long at mouth level, and form delicately-coloured plumes. Some types of tiny shell-fish choose to live in these plumes, where they find food and shelter.

How do oysters make pearls?

When you are a mollusc your main problem is that of protecting your soft body. In addition to its mantle of skin, the **oyster** is encased in a tough limy shell with two valves. If its outside is dull and rough, the inside is smooth and shiny so as not to harm the animal.

Throughout the seasons the oyster's mantle secretes successive layers of **mother of pearl**. These then line the shell. If a tiny animal happens to get into the shell it will soon be covered with a layer of mother of pearl—unless it is a quick mover.

So a pearl is a kind of reaction to the irritation of tiny parasites that get lodged in the oyster's mantle. The irritation causes the secretion of mother of pearl to increase.

How many types of pearl are there?

Pearls have a great variety of colours: from pure **white** to **black**, via **yellow**, **pink**, **blue** and **grey**. They are not all round in shape, and round pearls are in fact the rarest sort. The Japanese

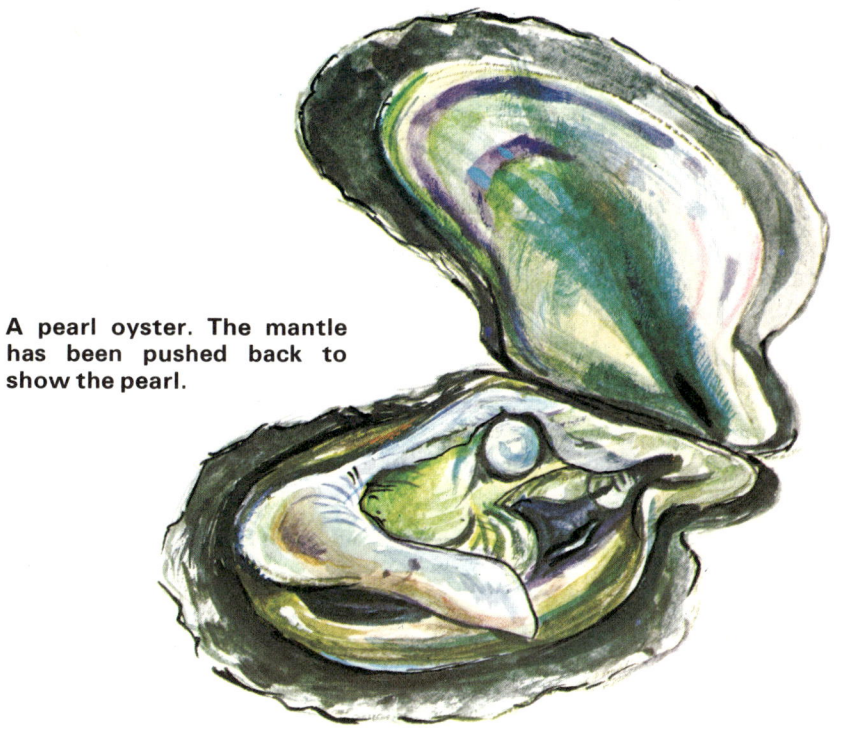

A pearl oyster. The mantle has been pushed back to show the pearl.

have long practised the art of making oysters form pearls by binding the mantle around a tiny glass ball. The pearls made in this way are known as cultured pearls.

Can mussels make pearls too?

Just like the oyster, the **mussel** is a mollusc. It too is protected by a bi-valve shell. It can also react to irritation by forming a pearl around the parasite, but the mussel's 'mother of pearl' is far less beautiful than the oyster's. The pearls it produces are small and not very pretty.

A mussel clings onto rocks by means of fibres produced by a gland in its foot. When there is no longer enough food in the surrounding area, the mussel breaks these fibres and crawls on its foot to another anchorage.

A mussel breeder gathering them in.

How does a shell-fish use jet propulsion to move about?

How can you move if you are encased in a shell?

The snail puts out its head, and has a broad foot to crawl on. But the oyster, the scallop and the carpet shell **have no head,** and their bi-valve shells look rather unwieldy.

The oyster has solved the problem by staying fixed to the same rock. The clam, which prefers black, muddy sand, has a **foot shaped like a shovel.** It can use this foot to dig a hole in the sand by pushing it through the gap between the two halves of its shell, and so find a quick hiding-place. As for the scallop, it moves through the water by opening and closing very rapidly.

Do scallops have jet propulsion?

On each side of the hinge small folds in the shell form **small nozzles.** Out of these the water shoots out like the gases at the back of a jet engine. And it knows very well where it is going. **The hundred or so tiny green eyes** around the edge of its mantle make sure of that.

Scallops can escape star-fish, who are very fond of them, thanks to a means of rapid propulsion.

All animals with a radula are molluscs, but some mulluscs do not have one of these rasping tongues. Neither the mussel nor the oyster has one, for example. The microscopic creatures that they eat do not really need 'grating'.

From top to bottom: Murex louedai, Lambis arthritica and Conus cedo. Although these shell-fish are beautiful they are all poisonous.

Are there poisonous shell-fish?

Molluscs with a single shell and their stomach in their foot—**the gasteropods**—have a remarkable tongue which specialists call the **radula.** It is like a highly-developed file whose teeth can be all sorts of shapes: from those with a tip as sharp as a needle, to those in the form of a fish-hook. Some gasteropods pierce the shells of other molluscs with this tongue. It unwinds like a ribbon, and **teeth are replaced** as they wear down.

Behind the **radula** in poisonous shell-fish there is a sack containing venom, and next to this is a pocket where the harpoon-like teeth are made. When the animal is hunting or defending itself it **fires these poisonous harpoons.** In this way it can kill the small fish and the worms on which it feeds.

Can they harm humans?

Careless shell-collectors who have been attracted by their large size and beautiful colours have occasionally fallen victim to these poisonous gasteropods. Some have died from the sting, others have been very ill. However, the six poisonous species are not found in the northerly regions. They live in the tropical reefs of the Pacific and Indian Oceans.

Why was the shell-fish called murex so precious in ancient times?

In ancient times the Greeks, Romans, Phoenicians and Egyptians kept the precious secretion of the **murex** exclusively for their idols, kings and dignitaries. These spiny-shelled gasteropod molluscs have in their linings a gland that produces a white milky liquid. When subjected to light the liquid turns yellow, then green, and finally purple. To make **one gramme of dye** you need **ten thousand murex.** That explains why it was even more valuable than gold. Veritable factories were built to treat these shell-fish.

There are also species of dye-producing murex on the coasts of America. Nowadays Mexican Indians extract the purple without killing the mollusc. It is a long and difficult operation, and requires a great deal of patience on the part of the Indians.

Despite their name, the shell-fish called 'purple' (the purpura, or dog whelk) do not provide purple dye. They get this name because of the shades they can be. There are no spines on its shell as there are on the murex's.

This spiky shell-fish is a Murex of the Troschelli species.

A giant clam firmly anchored on the rocky bottom.

Which is the biggest of all shell-fish?

The biggest of the shell molluscs is the **giant clam.** Its two valves can measure more than a yard across at the widest point and can be three inches thick. In a clam of this size the shell and the animal together reach a weight of **550 pounds** (250 kg.).

This enormous shell-fish lives on the bottom of the tropical Pacific Ocean. It keeps the valve opening gently inclined towards the surface. Although it lives on the small algae that grow within its shell, it is known as the **'man-eater'.**

How dangerous is the giant clam?

Terrible stories are told about it. Divers who brushed against its lining are said to have had a hand or a foot caught as the shell closed. This defensive closing is a reaction common to all bi-valves. Since it takes a great deal of effort to open even a small oyster, it can be easily imagined how a man trapped like this would find it impossible to prise open the shell.

Pearl-fishers are said to have cut off their hands or their feet rather than drown in this way. These stories are perhaps only fiction, but it is true that these molluscs do make pearls as big as **ping-pong balls.** Unfortunately they are dull and not iridescent, and have nothing more than simple 'curiosity value'.

Why do cuttle-fish spit ink?

When frightened, the cuttle-fish moves off backwards—throwing out ink as it goes.

Man has been using the ink from the **cuttle-fish** for a very long time now. The Chinese are said to have been the first to use it in this way. But the cuttle-fish does not make this liquid just for the benefit of the artists in the world. It uses it to defend, or more exactly, to hide itself. Already a master of the **art of camouflage,** since it can change its colour according to that of the sea-bed, it can throw out **a cloud of ink** by a contraction of its whole body and so obscure the enemy's view. At the same time this contraction expels the water that had passed into the ventral pouch, and the animal shoots backwards. It is rather like a jet aeroplane letting off coloured smoke.

A Chinese scholar drawing characters with a brush dipped in 'cuttle-fish ink' . . . Marking ink is often sold in small sticks that need to be dissolved in water before being used. They can be rubbed with a damp brush for doing wash-drawings.

31

How do sea-urchins move along?

It is a commonly believed fallacy that sea urchins can only use their spines for moving along. In fact **sea urchins** have feet, hundreds of little thread-like, soft and translucent feet with a sucker on the end. A series of ducts links the feet together and, tentacle-like, they swell with water and can reach double the length of the spines. The suckers stick to the rocks, and the sea urchin moves forward, one foot at a time, by using its spines like crutches.

A sea urchin's jaws have five long teeth. It uses them to browse on the algae growing on the rock it is moving over. Common sea urchin.

How can a star-fish eat an oyster?

Star-fish eat shell-fish, and are especially fond of oysters. Opening them, however, is no small matter. A **very strong muscle** holds the two halves of an oyster's shell tight together.

The star-fish has a novel way of overcoming this problem. Holding firmly onto the rock with two of its arms, with the other three it **pulls** with all its might on the top half of the oyster's shell. As soon as a small gap appears, the star-fish regurgitates its stomach, just like turning the **finger of a glove** inside out. All the tiny glands on the stomach's mucous membrane secrete a liquid that **digests the oyster** on the spot. The star-fish then has little trouble in opening the shell completely, and swallowing its own stomach along with the juice of the predigested oyster.

The great strength of the star-fish enables it to open even the most stubborn oyster.

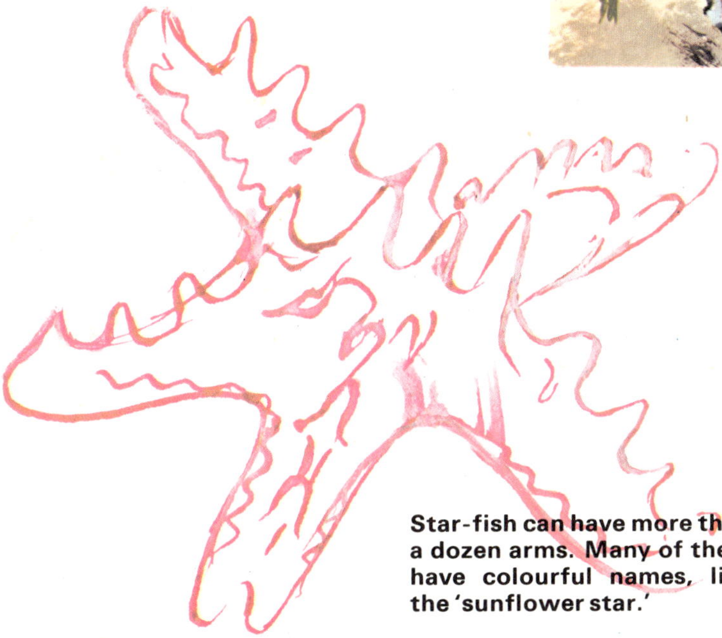

Star-fish can have more than a dozen arms. Many of them have colourful names, like the 'sunflower star.'

Is the sea cucumber really an animal?

Despite its name, the sea cucumber is well and truly an animal, and a cousin of the sea urchin and the star-fish. It is shaped like a **big gherkin** and is pinkish in colour. The tree-like tentacles around its mouth make it appear somewhat like a vegetable. Five double rows of tentacles, which it uses for walking, are like the bumps on a gherkin. In sea cucumbers the test (shell) that makes up the inner skeleton of sea urchins and star-fish is reduced to **minute** plates that are spread throughout the skin (ossicles).

A sea cucumber.

The sea cucumber is one of the Holothurians. Along with sea urchins, sea stars and crinoids, the holothuria make up the large family of echinoderms, or animals with a spiny skin. Unlike most animals they have things by fives rather than by twos. Thus the sea urchin has five jaws and five reproductive glands; sea stars have five digestive pockets.

When the animal is attacked it contracts violently, and throws out a mass of sticky threads that strangle the enemy.

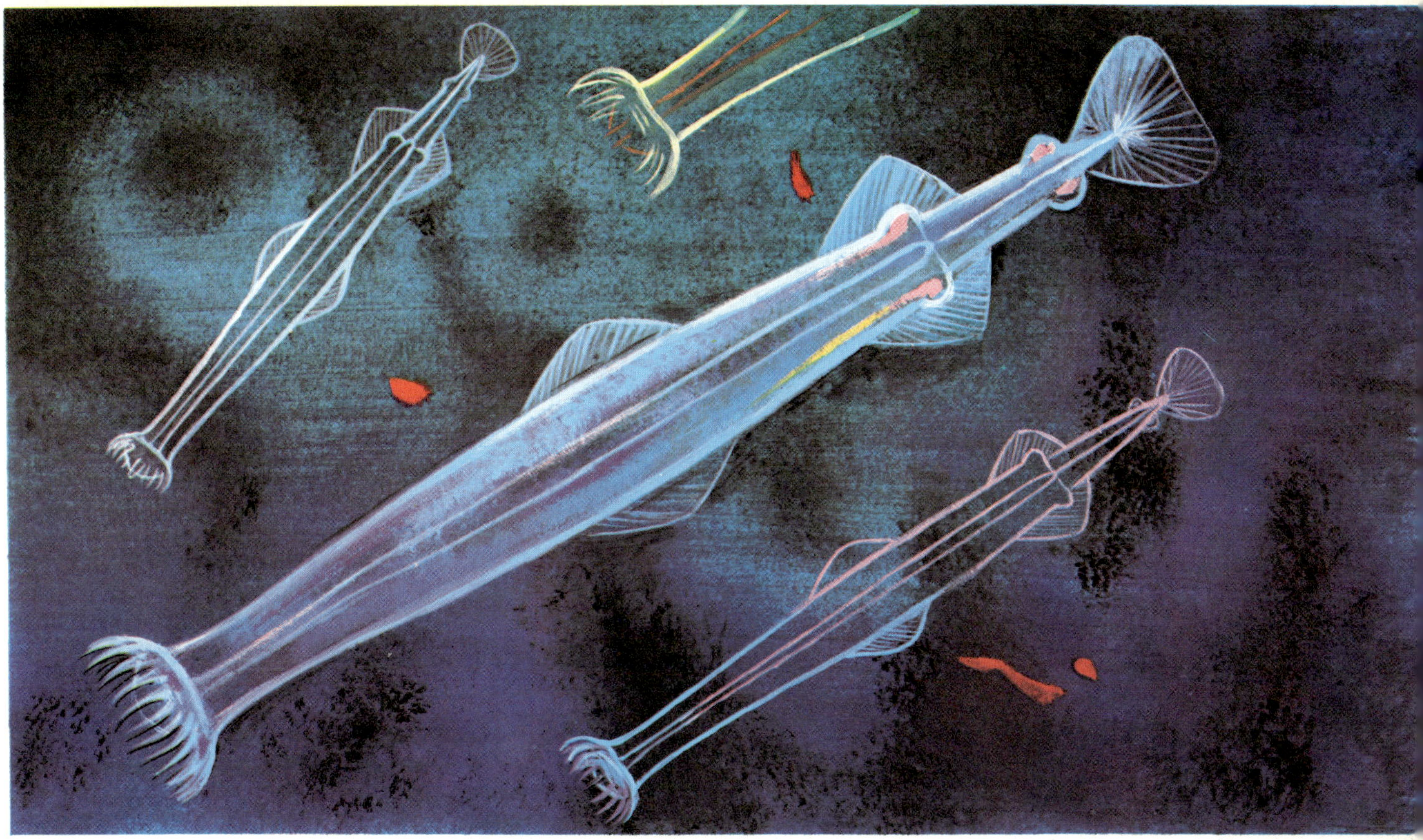

Are arrow worms really worms?

Sometimes in the plankton that fish eat there can be found astonishing quantities of tiny, transparent thread-like animals with lateral fins. These fins make them look like feathered arrows. Despite their appearance, they are not worms but **chaetognatha.** This is a difficult zoological group to classify, but it has certainly evolved further than worms and molluscs. It has, for example, a real tail like the vertebrates. The translation of their name, which comes from two Greek words, is roughly: 'bristle-jaws'. On either side of their mouths they do in fact have curved hairs with which they catch their prey.

'Arrow worms' are at once male and female. This is what is meant by being hermaphrodite. They lay their eggs in the sea. These eggs are fertilized in the animal's body before being laid. There are also herma-phrodite species of worm, and this has often led to the confusion of 'arrow worms' with worms.

Are the small transparent barrels found in plankton plants or animals?

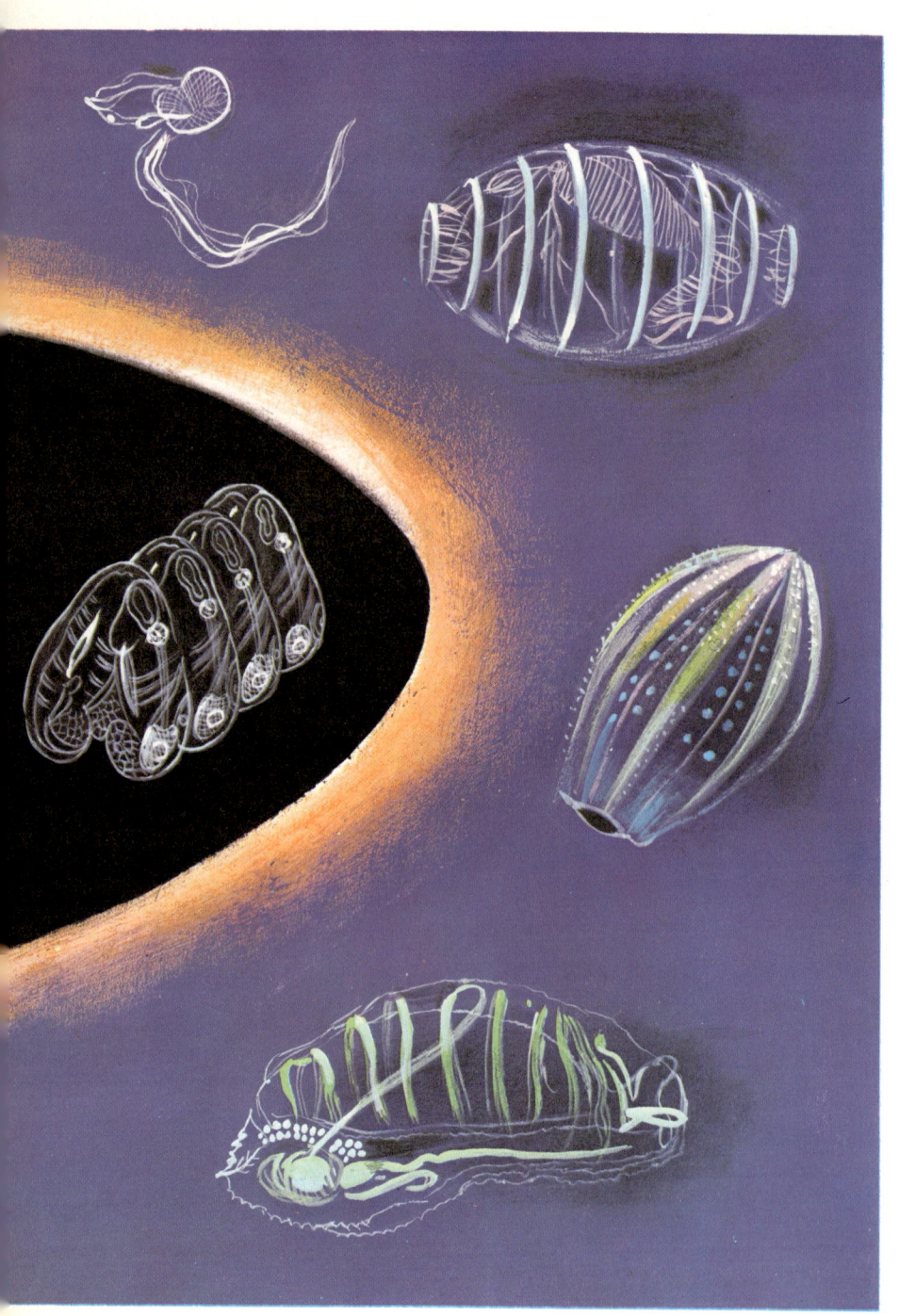

About half an inch long and with white stripes around them, these strange creatures are animals and, what is more, they are **fairly close to the vertebrates!** They are sometimes thought to be a kind of jelly-fish. The experts, however, assure us that they are a stage in the evolution of animals towards their most important characteristic: a spinal nervous system. **Salpae,** as they are called, move forward by a rhythmic contraction of their muscles. The effect of this is to **expel the water** from the respiratory sack which is at the back of the animal. More jet-propelled marine animals!

How do they reproduce?

Doliola are also members of this group. Salpae and doliola have a strange way of reproducing. Some of them are sexed, and they lay eggs. The eggs develop into asexual animals which reproduce by means of buds. The buds give rise to sexed animals. Sometimes these buds remain attached to each other and so form **strings** of young salpae.

Top left: tailed doliola larva. Top right: asexual adult doliola. Left centre: string of sexed young salpae. Right centre: sea gooseberry, a kind of jelly-fish that is easy to confuse with the salpae. Bottom: asexual adult salpa.

CRUSTACEA

What are the strange transparent shapes that can be seen
swimming under the water?

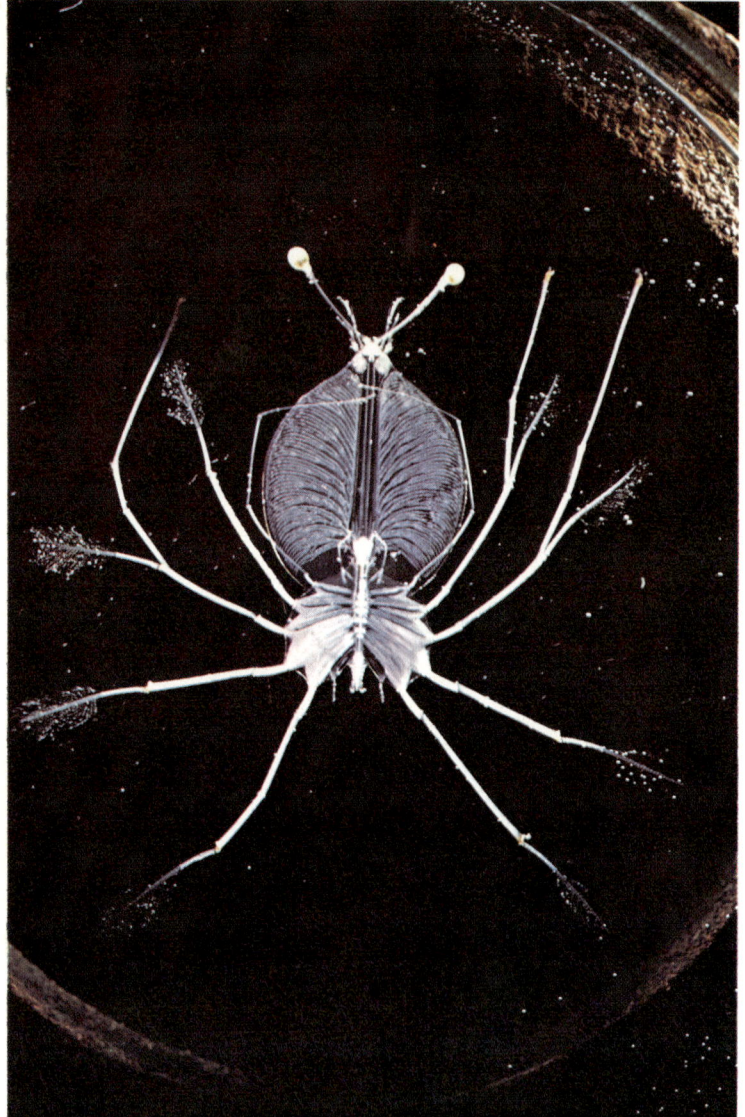

What are those strange transparent shapes that we see swimming around in great numbers in certain shallow rocky waters? They are unbelievably flat and translucent, moving along with their **thread-like legs.** They look rather like leaves and have **globular** eyes at the end of long stems. These baby spiny lobsters are very different from their parents as they can pass through the clear water almost like ghosts. The magnificent tail which for us is a delicacy is at this stage nothing more than a spine at the end of an unusual body.

How does it develop?

There will have to be many changes before the larvae can become adult spiny lobsters. The transformation will be almost as dramatic as that which changes a caterpillar into a butterfly.

Like a small boy who changes his short pants for long trousers, the animal changes its outer covering several times during its childhood. But, unlike man, who stops growing when he has reached adulthood, it will continue to grow until it dies, **discarding its shell** every time it becomes too small.

People often confuse the lobster and the spiny lobster. It is not very difficult to tell the difference, however. The lobster has two enormous claws. The spiny lobster has none, but its head bristles with spines and two very long antennae give it a very different appearance.

What does a spiny lobster use its magnificent antennae for?

Like all crustacea, the spiny lobster breathes through gills. When you pull a leg off a cooked spiny lobster you can often see things looking like grey feathers coming out. These are the animal's gills. They are hidden under the shell covering the head and the thorax.

It is natural to think that the spiny lobster would be easier to approach than the lobster with its **huge claws,** but that is far from the truth. It can kill or tear open its enemies with one blow from its **rough spiny antennae.**

All crustacea have two pairs of antennae. The first pair is quite small and is used for feeling, touching and tasting. The others are also used for touching but they can also at times be used for defence.

Finally, at the base of each of the spiny lobster's great antennae, there is a **small hole** through which it passes its urine.

A fishmonger showing his wares. He is holding a special trap for catching large crustacea.

Is a big crab older than a small one?

If both the crabs are of the same species then the big one is older than the small one. Crabs grow all their lives. They change their **shells** regularly. The shell that protects their soft fragile bodies is impregnated with limestone. This makes it a very hard crust indeed —hence the name of crustacea which is given to crabs and related species with shells. But the hard covering does not grow with the animal, and when the animal grows it has to dispense with its now undersized shell. It must then grow rapidly before the new shell formed by its skin becomes too rigid. It has to do this as quickly as possible because the shell hardens in a very short time, and also because it is defenceless during the period of change. So it swells up with water and hides as best it can.

Is it important to know the difference?

When you buy a fresh crab it is a good thing to be able to distinguish the ones that have just **shed** their shells from those who have had them for a good length of time. If you choose the former you will end up with an animal that has very little flesh and a great deal of water in it—and is therefore far less appetizing.

The big edible crab is a rather amorphous creature. In certain regions it is called the 'sleeper'.

The commonest crab on our shores is the small green or 'shore' crab.

When you look at a crab's mouth you can see a whole mass of flat instruments moving at great speed. These are the animal's mouthpieces. The crab has six pairs of instruments for holding, masticating and pulverizing its prey: small legs, jaws and mandibles.

Is the barnacle a mushroom, a shell-fish or a crustacean?

Sometimes strange creatures can be seen on driftwood: from a distance they look like mushrooms, and from close up they look like shell-fish. You have to go back to the first days of their lives to discover that they are in fact crustaceans. Their larvae are similar to those of other crustaceans, but the tiny antennae already have on them the discs with which they will attach themselves at a later stage.

The antennae will eventually disappear, and the animal's whole body is deformed by its life of clinging to objects. The area in front of the mouth extends to become the peduncle; the thorax is enclosed in a suit of protective plates, and the abdomen disappears. Its thoracic appendages, which are no longer feet but hairs (cilia), gather the animal's food.

Barnacles attached to a piece of driftwood.

Are sand-hoppers insects?

Although they jump rather like the fleas you may find on cats and dogs, this is where the resemblance with such insects comes to an end.

They look more like tiny shrimps with legs going out in all directions. Like the shrimp, the crab, the lobster and the spiny lobster, sand-hoppers are crustaceans that live in a **hinged** shell similar to a suit of armour.

They are harmless creatures: they curl up in holes that they dig in moist sand. Their **tiny blue eyes** bring a touch of colour to their shells which merge with the colour of the sand.

Under a pile of seaweed that is drying slowly in the sunshine, hundreds of sand-hoppers can be found busily looking for the microscopic animals they feed on.

In the water they are good, fast swimmers—and they have to be to escape their many enemies, for whom they are something of a **delicacy.**

A sand-hopper.

The parasitic barnacle: a problem solved at long last?

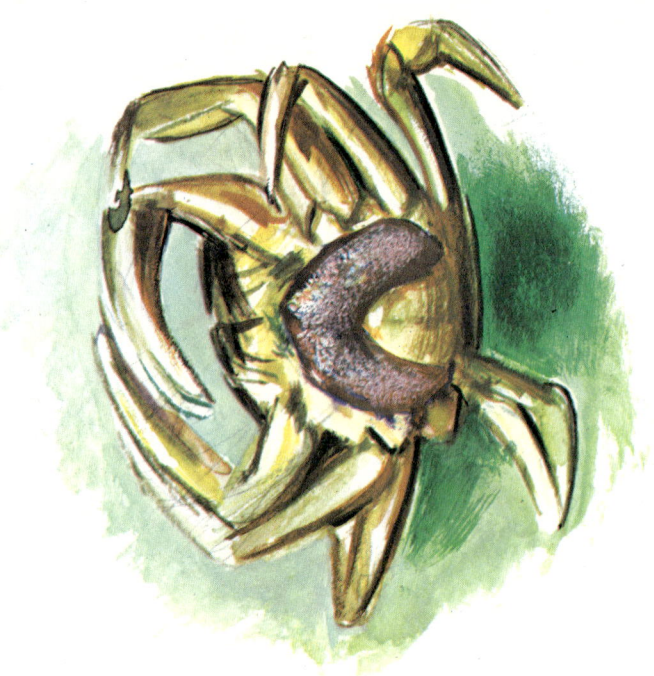

What is the **large pink bag** on the underside of this crab—a swollen tumour?

For a long time this was a mystery to zoologists. As in the case of the ordinary barnacle, you have to go back to the beginning of their larval existence to see that it is actually a species of crustacean! The swimming larva which is typical of the crustacea quickly makes its way into the crab through the base of one of its small antennae, and then **attaches itself to the intestines.** It then undergoes an amazing transformation. The parasitic life turns it into a tangle of roots anchored inside the crab, and a large bag!

Is there such a thing as a feathered crustacean?

The crustacean most frequently found in plankton is a **tiny creature** no more than one-tenth to one-eighth of an inch (2 to 3mm.) long. It moves by flapping its long antennae that fold back along its body. They are called **copepoda.** The antennae, which are sometimes two or three times the length of the body, often end in sorts of coloured feathers or pom-poms: these make them one of the wonders of nature.

The tail can also be decorated with a trail of very long 'feathers'.

The most iridescent species are to be found in warm waters, but the others flourish everywhere and are a much sought-after food for fish and whales. A quantity of copepoda fried in butter is said to be delicious . . .

FISH

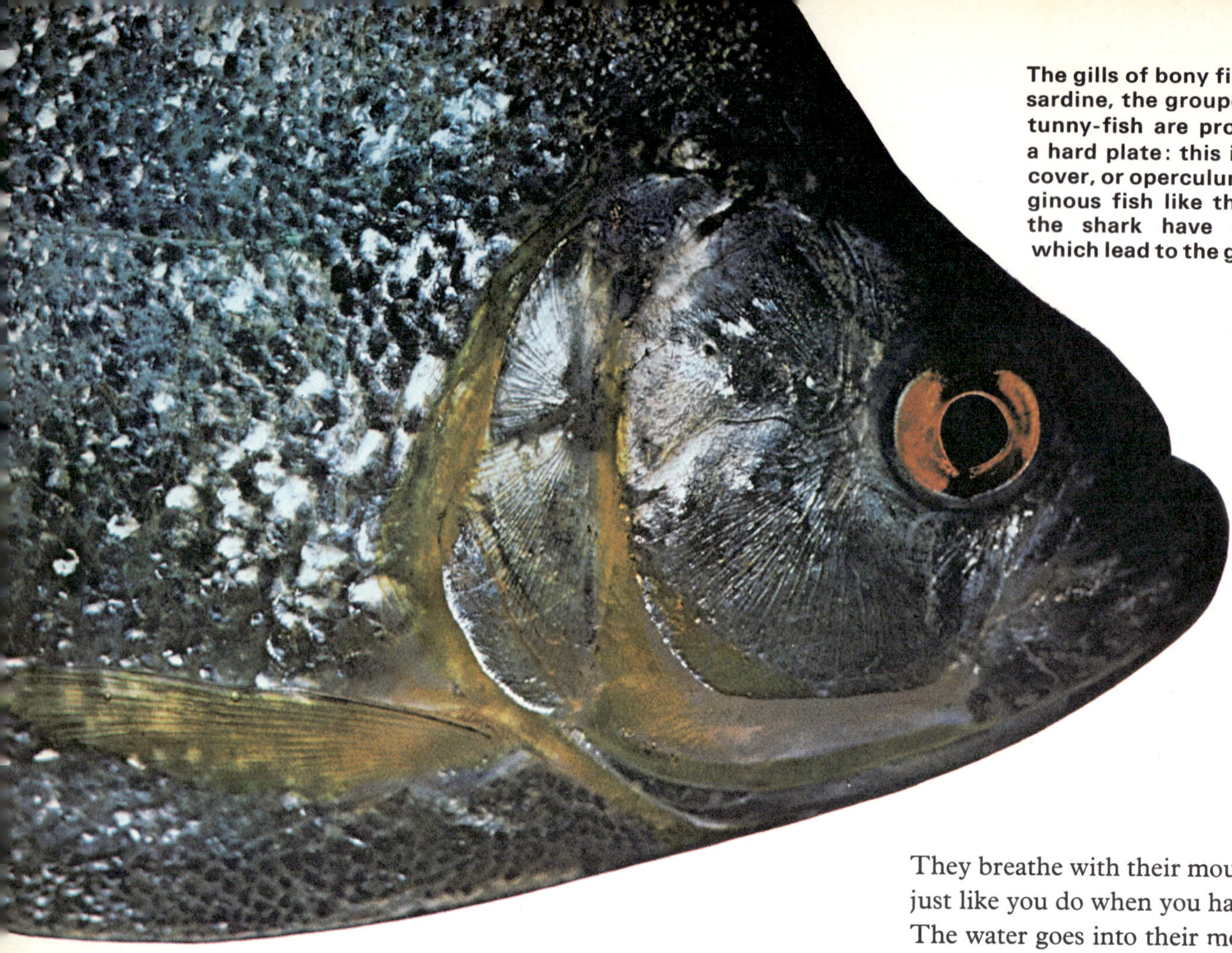

The gills of bony fish like the sardine, the grouper and the tunny-fish are protected by a hard plate: this is the gill-cover, or operculum. Cartilaginous fish like the ray and the shark have only slits which lead to the gills.

How do fish breathe?

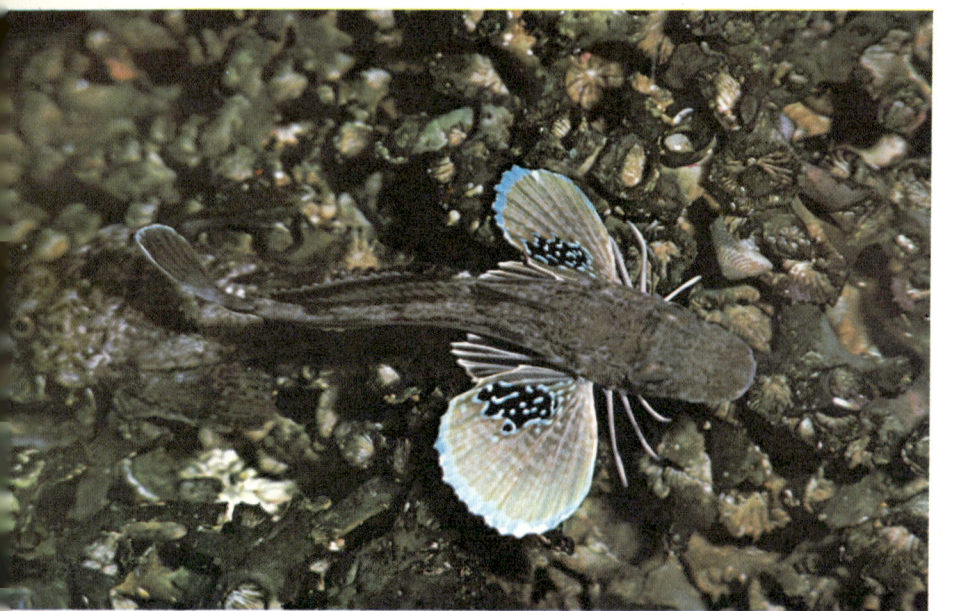

A gurnard can quite easily stay half an hour out of the water.

They breathe with their mouths open, just like you do when you have a cold. The water goes into their mouths and comes out through the gills. Water is thus channelled through the **gills** in which the blood circulates. The oxygen in the water passes through the gills into the blood vessels, and the carbonic gas comes in the reverse direction. There is, however, one family of fish—the **dipneusti**—that as well as gills have a pair of lungs with which they can take in air directly. These fish can only be found in the swamps and rivers of tropical Africa and tropical America. There are none of them in the sea.

The sea fish that come out of the water to hunt or to bask in the sunshine breathe through their gills, which they keep moist by closing the gill-covers. They would die fairly soon if the stayed too long out of the water.

How can a fish stay at the same level without having to move?

Those who like swimming underwater are well aware of the effort needed to stop themselves from floating up to the surface. But the small rock fish that we can see underwater does not seem to have to make any great effort to stay at a chosen level. It can stay at the depth it likes without moving a single fin—just like a submarine.

What are the similarities?

The submarine and the fish are in fact working on the same principle. Just as a submarine has **ballast-tanks** that take in the required weight of water for a given depth, the fish has an **air-bladder** which contains air more or less according to the depth. But some fish have no air-bladder: sharks and rays, for example, do not have one and like us have to move continually to stay at the same depth.

A longspine squirrelfish in its coral reef.

The outline of this submarine has been designed so that it will give the least resistance possible to the water it has to go through. Its 'nose' is, for this reason, very similar to the sperm whale's.

Can fish hear?

Fish have **no ears we can see,** nor any eardrums. However, they can still pick up noises that pass through the water. The sound vibrations are picked up by the whole body and transmitted to the **internal ear,** which is inside the skull.

Some fish families have very keen hearing. In these species the air-bladder picks up the sounds. The sounds are then passed to the internal ear by a series of tiny bones, in the same way that the chain of bones in a man's ear—the stirrup-bone, the anvil and the hammer—link the ear-drum to the receiving organs in the brain.

Experiments have shown that fish can **recognize different kinds of sounds.** The best results are obtained with the fish that hear through their air-bladder.

With fish that live in groups, it has been observed that they occasionally give out signals which determine the behaviour of the whole group.

However, some species are either partially or totally deaf; this is probably because the conditions in which they live make hearing an unnecessary sense, and it has declined while another sense—that of sight or smell—has reached a higher stage of development.

A shoal of butterfly fish. In the face of any danger they all turn back simultaneously, imitating those in front.

Top: A red goby from the coast of California.
Bottom: A drum fish from the West Indies.

Are fish mute?

It is quite incorrect to think that fish cannot produce sounds. Many fish communicate to form shoals, to come together at mating time or to frighten enemies. The noisiest of all fish is probably the **drum fish** from the east Atlantic. Fish give out sounds in a variety of ways: by beating their **gill-covers** or by grinding their teeth, for example. Some fish make their air-bladders vibrate, or let out the air in them with a hissing sound that can be heard even above the water.

How else can a fish produce sound?

Anything in a fish can be used to make a noise, even the skeleton. Trigger-fish, for instance, use the bones that attach their pectoral fins; sheat-fish, who look like eels with moustaches, **rattle** their vertebrae vigorously when caught.

But fish are real specialists in the realm of ultrasonics: the people who first used **sonars** were amazed to hear the number of ultrasonic sounds produced by fish.

Fish are quite able to communicate with their fellows. Some fish have mating dances very much like those performed by birds. The male comes up to the female and remains motionless for a second; it then tries to impress her by swimming around as gracefully as it can. Sometimes the female joins in. They link their pectoral fins together and move quickly up towards the surface; they then dive to the bottom where the female lays her eggs, which are then fertilized by the male.

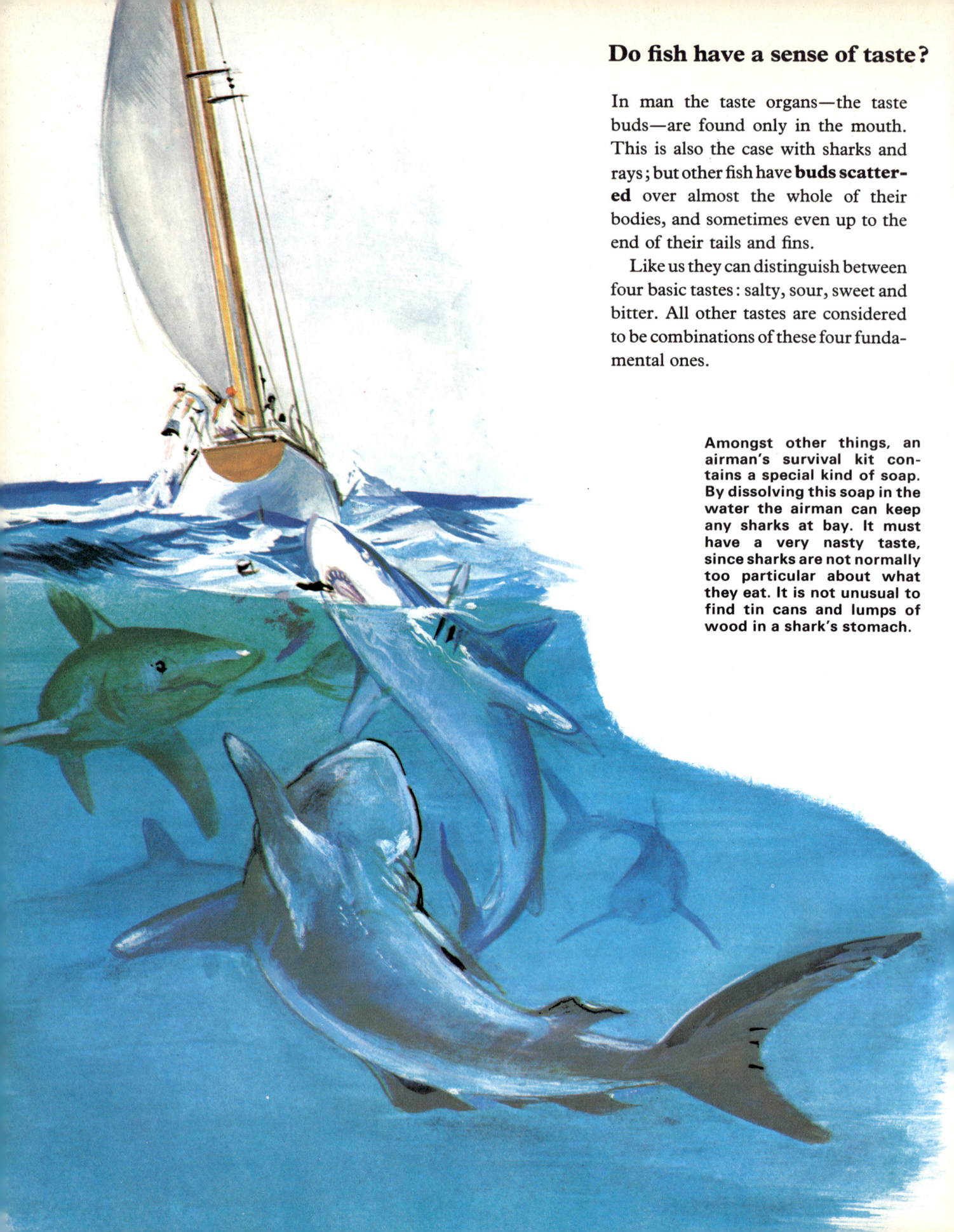

Do fish have a sense of taste?

In man the taste organs—the taste buds—are found only in the mouth. This is also the case with sharks and rays; but other fish have **buds scattered** over almost the whole of their bodies, and sometimes even up to the end of their tails and fins.

Like us they can distinguish between four basic tastes: salty, sour, sweet and bitter. All other tastes are considered to be combinations of these four fundamental ones.

Amongst other things, an airman's survival kit contains a special kind of soap. By dissolving this soap in the water the airman can keep any sharks at bay. It must have a very nasty taste, since sharks are not normally too particular about what they eat. It is not unusual to find tin cans and lumps of wood in a shark's stomach.

Do fish have a good sense of smell?

Salmon on their way upstream. To get through rapids they often have to jump very high.

All fish have broad nostrils which are not used for breathing but for smelling. They link the outside with **large nasal sacks** where the ends of the olfactory nerves open out. These terminate in large round lumps in the brain which are often far bigger than the brain proper. This gives an indication of how extremely important the sense of smell is for fish.

The shark owes its prowess as a hunter to its **extraordinarily acute sense of smell.** It will rush in for the kill even if the tell-tale drop of blood is over a hundred yards away.

A salmon can recognize the river in which it was born **thanks to its sense of smell.** It has also been shown that its 'nose' is sensitive to solutions whose concentrations are the equivalent of dissolving **one nine thousandth of an ounce** of a substance in Lake Geneva!

A grouper from the Red Sea in its coral home.

Do fish sleep?

When you sleep you close your eyes— or, more exactly, the lids close over your eye-balls like small curtains. But this is not the eyelids' main function. They are continuously moving up and down to moisten the eye. Since fish live in water they **have no need of lids** to keep their eyes moist, and consequently have no lids at all. But they still rest like all living animals, during the day or the night according to their particular habits. They have no need to lie down to rest: having chosen their spot, all they have to do is to float in the water. The sea is a dangerous place to live in, and it must be easier to avoid a surprise attack if your eyes stay open —even if you are asleep!

50

Which is the world's biggest fish?

The world's biggest fish is a shark that lives in the warmer regions of the ocean. It can be as much as **50 feet long** (18m.) and weigh **15 tons.** Its size and weight have brought it the name of whale-shark.

It is a rather apathetic animal, and to catch food it just swims along with its mouth wide open. It lives on plankton and small fish. It loves to laze in the sunshine, and to do this comes into shallower waters where it can find a comfortable bed of sand. Not surprisingly it is an easy fish to catch, and can be harpooned and heaved on board without offering the slightest resistance. Its eggs are the **biggest in the animal world:** even bigger than the ostrich's. It is possible to argue that its apathy and its scarcity are symptoms of a species on the road to extinction.

A whale-shark.

Will a shark eat anything?

Sharks are unbelievably greedy animals. This is coupled with a high degree of insensitivity. Whether they are big or small they have phenomenal appetites: **bottles and even tin cans** have been found in their stomachs. They follow boats to pick up any kitchen waste that may be thrown overboard. So they have always been an unwelcome fellow-traveller for sailors. It was an unlucky man who fell overboard.

Not all sharks are man-eating, however. Above all they prefer fish, but are so greedy that they can be tempted to eat a man if he is smaller than they are. This nasty disposition, coupled with their razor-sharp teeth, make them feared and hated in those parts of the world where they are likely to come close to the shore.

Does a shark often lose its teeth?

The shark has large **triangular** teeth with jagged edges. They are fairly thin and have only tiny roots that sink one-fifth of their total height into the jaws. Being a voracious animal, the shark often breaks teeth or pulls up the roots when dealing with a tough-skinned victim. They also get blunt very quickly.

The best way of keeping the shark well supplied with sharp teeth was Nature's answer of giving it **renewable teeth.** Its teeth fan outwards from the jaw-bone, and the tooth in use is the one highest up in the row. Worn teeth gradually fall outwards. Sharks lose their teeth like other animals lose their fur or their feathers: that is, in order to renew them. This ability to replace worn and blunted teeth is another reason for the shark's fearsome reputation as a hunter.

You have to admire the courage of the photographer —even if he was protected by a metal cage as this shark came in for the kill.

To get hold of its prey a shark has to turn onto its side. It has to rotate slightly, since its mouth is on the underside of its head.

What is a sea eagle?

The sea eagle is not a bird: it is also known as the eagle-fish, and is in fact the biggest of the rays—the **manta ray.** It is also called 'eagle-fish' because it can glide over the water for quite a distance. The horns on either side of its mouth make it look like an enormous **stag beetle.** It is the appearance of these horns that causes it to be called, on certain islands, the 'devil fish'.

Whatever name you care to give it, it is very adept at using its pectoral fins to channel small fish, swimming molluscs and crustacea towards the round flat teeth contained in its large mouth.

It inhabits the tropical waters of the Atlantic and the east Pacific. One of its smaller relations can be found in the Mediterranean and the east Atlantic.

The manta is the biggest of the rays. It is between sixteen and twenty feet long, and can jump more than six feet out of the water.

You can see how enormous the sea eagle really is when compared to a man.

54

What is a sea angel?

This heavenly name conceals a rather nasty-looking shark. However, the angel-fish is **harmless** as far as man is concerned: it eats small fish, crustacea and molluscs.

It gets its name from the two well-developed pectoral fins which look very much like wings. These also give it something of the appearance of a ray. But the **squatina,** as it is properly called, cannot flap its 'wings' as the ray can. They are only used as stabilizers when the fish is searching for prey very close to the sea-bed: it is the tail that propels it along.

There was a time when the sea angel was very plentiful in the bay on whose shore the French town of Nice is situated. Because of this, the bay is known to this day as the Bay of Angels.

A sea angel searching for molluscs on the sea-bed.

The sea angel does not lay its eggs: it keeps them in a cavity in its body until they hatch. The female gives birth to twenty little ones, between nine and twelve inches long. In the egg they live on food stored within the egg itself. This is very different from what happens in mammals, where the baby in the womb is linked to the mother by an umbilical cord. Everything necessary for its development passes through the cord.

If you catch a torpedo-ray in your net be careful not to touch it. Even when it is dying it can give you a strong electric shock. Take the case of a man out fishing for pleasure. He was bringing a net full of soles when he saw a torpedo-ray caught in the net. Taking great care not to touch it, he folded the net with the fish in it on the side of his boat. Unluckily, a lurch of the boat caused him to fall on the net and an electric shock sent him flying to the other end of the boat!

Why does the numb-fish give you an electric shock when you touch it?

Active nerve cells produce electricity. The current is very weak, but when there are a lot of **cells** together as there are in our brains, it is strong enough to be measured on an instrument called an electro-encephalograph.

The electricity produced by the brain of a ray—or **numbfish**—travels through its nerves to the muscles at the front of its lateral fins: here it accumulates. These muscles operate very much **like a battery in a car.** However, at the slightest touch the whole of the electricity accumulated in these muscles is discharged in one current. This stinging discharge would be enough to light a bulb or ring a bell. It takes the numbfish over a day to **recharge its batteries.**

Are there other 'electric' fish?

Other fish can also give electric shocks. In **stargazers**—angle-fish that bury themselves in the sand leaving only their eyes visible—the electric current travels via the **optic nerve** and accumulates in the eye muscles. In some species glands in the skin work as electrical accumulators.

The strongest discharge comes from a fresh-water fish—from the **electric eel,** which can even electrocute a man.

A mottled numbfish.

A stargazer.

An electric eel.

Why is cod-liver oil so good for our health?

Small fish like the herring and the sardine feed on plankton and especially on tiny animal or vegetable organisms that float on the surface in minute drops of oil. Being exposed to the sun, these droplets of oil contain large amounts of **vitamin A.** The **cod** eats vast quantities of small fish with greasy flesh. The excess grease consumed by the cod is stored in its liver, so it is not surprising that the oil extracted from the liver contains vitamin A, in addition to other highly nutritious substances.

Why do we need it?

A man's body, however, cannot make vitamin A on its own although it is vital for **renewing eye pigment,** for helping **heal** cuts and for combatting **infection.** So it has to find ready-made vitamin A in food: butter and milk contain some, for example, but cod-liver oil is the richest source. It does not taste very nice of course, but nowadays it is put into tiny tasteless capsules which then dissolve in the stomach.

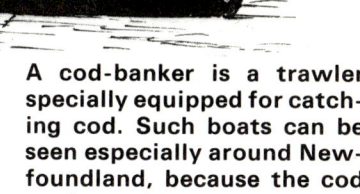

A cod-banker is a trawler specially equipped for catching cod. Such boats can be seen especially around Newfoundland, because the cod prefers colder waters.

A cod.

Cod are very prolific fish. Every mating season a female can lay up to nine million eggs! When they come out of the egg the small fry are one-fifteenth to one-tenth of an inch long; under their stomachs there is a large bag stocked with food since it cannot feed itself yet. The bag disappears after several days. When the fish is about one and one-twelfth inches long it moves into deeper water, going as far as fourteen hundred feet down, and stays there for several years.
Cod live in large shoals. In the north-east Atlantic they set off on long migrations in search of food.

What is caviar?

The tiny black balls that are so expensive, and are the delight of gourmets when served on buttered toast, are nothing more than fish eggs. But the fish from which they come is no ordinary one: the **sturgeon** is found mainly in the briny waters of certain river mouths. It is a very powerful animal, and can swim up fast-flowing rivers like the Volga and the Danube. Some species of sturgeon can weigh more than 3,000 pounds (1,400 kg.). A female can produce up to 220 pounds (100 kg.) of eggs

They can be taken out of a dead sturgeon, or out of a living one by squeezing the belly of a female sturgeon that is about to lay. The sturgeon is then put back in the water. Before they are packaged the outer membrane is removed and they are dipped in pickling brine. For fish specialists—**ichthyologists**—the sturgeon represents an intermediate stage between fish with cartilaginous skeletons, like the shark and the ray, and those with bony skeletons like the sardine, the tunny and the carp. The sturgeon's

The biggest of all sturgeons is the huso. It can be as much as thirty feet long and weigh nearly one and a half tons. It can be found in the Caspian, the Adriatic and the Black Seas. It also goes up the rivers that flow into these seas.

Caviar is not the only thing that a sturgeon provides. A kind of glue can also be made from it, called fish-glue, or isinglass.

skeleton is in fact half cartilaginous and half bony.

It is very sensitive to polluted water, and the already high price of caviar can only go up as sturgeon get rarer and rarer.

Fishing for sturgeon in the south of the Caspian Sea.

Why are soles white on one side and brown on the other?

The **sole** is a strange, very flat fish. Both its eyes are on the same side of its body, and because it could not possibly swim normally, due to its extreme thinness, it always lays on the side that has no eyes and wafts through shallow waters like a leaf in the wind.

When it is tired or wishes to elude a pursuer it rests on the sea-bed and changes colour to match it. When you are exposed to sun-light your skin grows darker because tiny black grains —**pigments**—come to the surface of the skin. The resulting sun-tan helps to protect you from the sun.

How does it change colour?

A sole's skin also contains pigments, and these arrange themselves over the side with the eyes on it according to the colour of the sea-bed it happens to be on. Since the pigments always colour the same side, the other side remains white. Zoologists once tried an interesting experiment: a sole was placed on a **draught-board.** After a short while the top side of the fish began to look like a draught-board! This phenomenon is called **mimicry:** the sole imitates the colour of the sea bottom it is laying on.

When the small sole comes out of its egg, it has eyes on either side of its head like all fish. Only when it grows up will one of the eyes move closer to the other. This applies to the eyes of all flat fish like the sole, the plaice or the dab.

Who painted these strange fish?

In the shallow waters of warmer parts of the oceans, there can often be found **beautifully coloured** fish. Their frequently odd-shaped bodies are striped with colours such as orange, yellow and blue. Their tails or mouths are often splashed with vivid colours: many of them even look as though they had lipstick on. But Nature has endowed them with this beauty for a very practical purpose—survival.

Trigger-fish have a great variety of different colourings. When they are frightened the rays of their front dorsal fin stand on end. If a trigger-fish is hidden in the crack of a rock, it is almost impossible to pull it out, because it is wedged in by its rays.

How do they survive?

One species of trigger-fish has been named the **'Picasso fish'**: they feed mainly on crustacea whose shells they crush with their powerful teeth. Chaetodons also have a vast range of colourings, but complicate the expert's task even further by changing colour as they grow older!

All these coloured tropical fish can be seen in aquariums: at first sight it would seem that their exotic colouring is a sort of natural joke. But in fact their stripes and markings are effective **camouflage** in the brightly coloured coral reefs which are their natural habitat.

A 'Picasso-fish'.

Chaetodontida

Above: Trigger-fish.
Below: Acanthurus.

How do sea-horses swim?

With its fat stomach, its trumpet-shaped mouth and its bent neck, the **sea-horse** moves along by turning its dorsal fin like a propeller. It is the only fish to have a head at right angles to its body, and since it swims upright it has both a strange and a familiar look about it.

Its head is vaguely like a horse's (hence the name—the technical name is hippocampus, 'hippos' being the Greek word for a horse), and their carriage makes them look like the caricature of a person. The tail has no fins, but is very flexible and can grasp hold of the seaweed amongst which it prefers to live. The very small pectoral fins are of no use as far as movement is concerned. Only the rapid rotating action of the tiny dorsal fin helps the sea-horse to move slowly along.

The male sea-horse is a **dutiful father:** he collects the eggs laid by the female and keeps them in his ventral pouch until they hatch out. Hence it seems that the male of the species gives birth to the young!

A pensive sea-horse.

Is there such a thing as a walking fish?

The legs of frogs, reptiles and mammals have come from the ventral and pectoral fins of fish.
The bat-fish, which **walks** and jumps on its ventral and pectoral fins, is a forerunner of this evolution.

The fish is the master of the watery element through which it swims so easily and so gracefully. In addition, some species, while remaining excellent swimmers, are able to move along the sea-bed. The **bat-fish,** a close relation of the angler-fish, can crawl along 'on all fours' with the help of its pectoral and ventral fins. It can even jump like a frog.

As for the **gurnards,** with their huge heads, some of them have pectoral fins in which the three bottom rays are independent and moveable like thin insect legs. They use them for **climbing onto rocks** that jut out above the water, and stay there up to half an hour at a time, basking in the sunshine.

You may think this is a strange way for a fish to behave, but it is probably an indication of what happened in the distant past when animals, having conquered the sea, set out to explore the land—for reasons that were as irresistible as they were mysterious. As this exploration of the world outside the sea became more and more daring, some fish left the water forever and became solely 'land' animals.

Top left: Bat-fish from the Gulf of Mexico.
Above: Red gurnard.
Bottom left: Bull-head from the East Pacific.

The gurnard uses its free pectoral rays not only for walking on the sea bottom, but also for feeling its prey. The gurnard is a noisy fish with a characteristic grunt. Another 'groaner', the bull-head, can also walk but, unlike the gurnard, it is a poor swimmer.

Can flying fish fly?

If you go on a cruise in warm seas, you may be lucky enough to see some **flying fish.** In fact flying fish do not really fly. They jump out of the water —as do other fish—but their extremely long pectoral fins enable them to glide for about **ten seconds** and cover something like **a hundred yards.** They begin their flight well before they leave the water, by flicking their tails and swimming at an angle. The actual leap can take them onto the deck of a liner, since they can go very high but without much sense of direction. Some species also use their ventral fins to improve their flight.

Flying-fish occasionally move in shoals; they leap and glide, probably to avoid pursuers who must be rather surprised to see their prey disappear.

What are angler-fish?

There are some fish that use the same techniques as the fisherman.

Like him they use a rod, a line, a hook, and even some bait. Nature has given the **angler-fish** a dorsal fin that looks exactly like a fishing-rod. Attracted by the lantern shining at the end of the 'line', small fish find themselves covered in a sticky liquid coming from the glands at the end of the ray and helplessly disappear into the enormous, spiky mouth of the 'angler'.

Other deep-sea fish use **luminous bait** to attract their prey, and when men fish with lanterns they are only imitating them.

The angler-fish is medium-sized—between three and six feet long. In relation to its body, its head is enormous. It is extremely ugly, and fishmongers never put its head on show; its cousin from the great depths of the ocean is even more frightening because of its long, needle-sharp teeth.

What are deep-water fish like?

Beyond the sun's reach, in the great depths of the ocean, there can be found some fearsome-looking fish. Their mouths are huge in relation to their bodies, and the teeth in them are **long pointed daggers** curving backwards like those of a snake. They can swallow victims bigger than themselves, due to their flabby stomachs that stretch to an amazing size. Some of them are tall and rather flat, while others have snake-like bodies. Nearly all of them have **luminous organs** on their heads or bodies, and these bring glimmers of green and red light to the darkness.

Just how big are they?

Most of these **'monsters',** however, are no more than **three or so inches** long; and if their mouths are so big it is because there is so little food at these depths that they have to take what prey they can—irrespective of its size.

One of the biggest of these creatures has an enormous head and a long thread-like body: its overall length is about 22 inches.

The tiny monsters are occasionally paid a visit by remarkable swimmers about six feet long—lancet-fish: these gobble up large amounts of the small fish, and then go back near the surface to digest them.

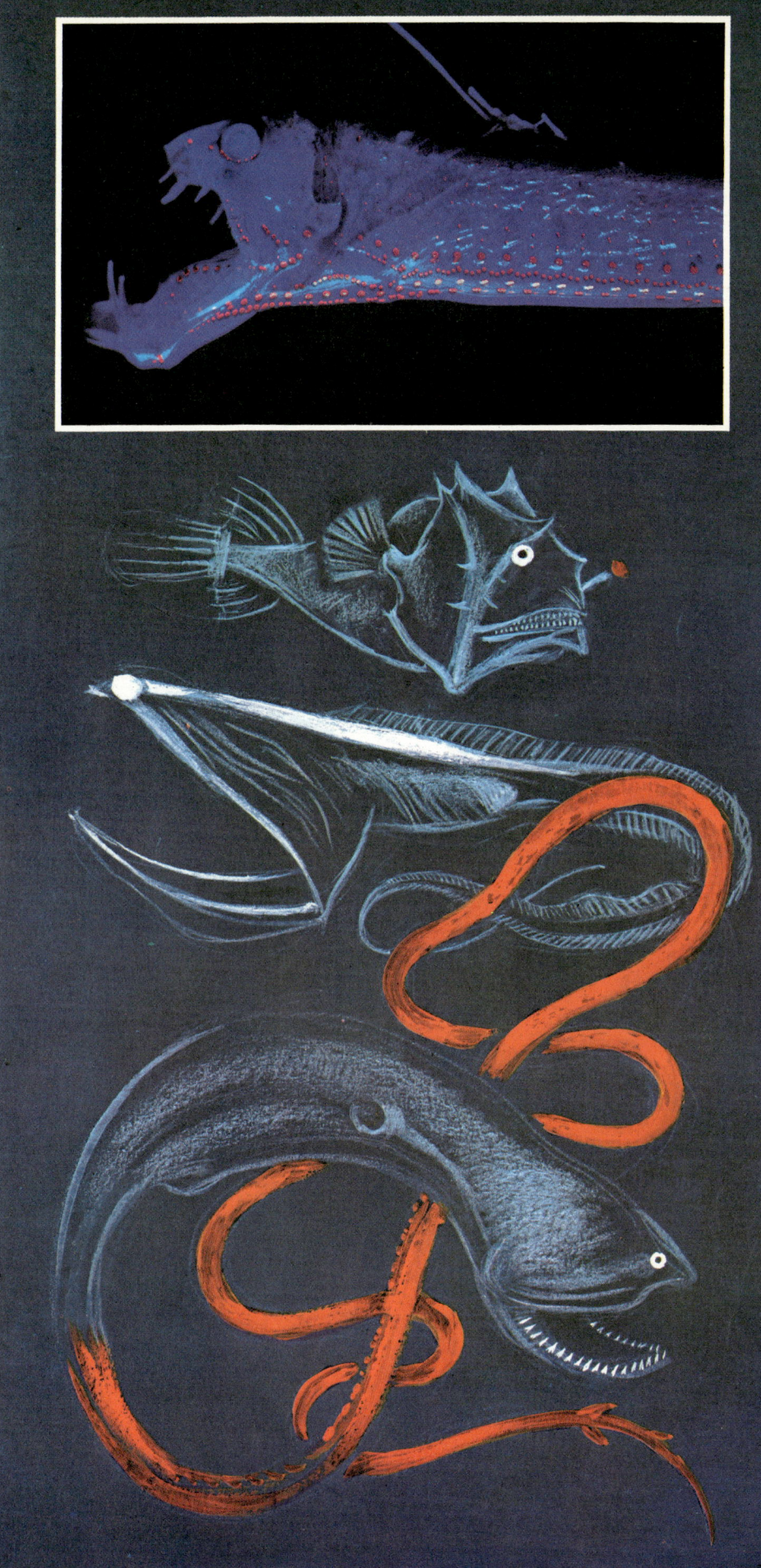

The photograph at the top of the page shows a luminous fish from the ocean deeps. The luminous organs are clearly visible due to being lit by ultra-violet light.

Are the fish down in the depths of the ocean blind?

Where total darkness reigns, animals lose their eyes. In the case of several species of fish and frogs that live in caves or underground streams where there is no light at all, the eyes declined and eventually disappeared altogether: they had become useless. When an organ falls into disuse because it is no longer necessary or useful for the animal's survival, it is said to 'atrophy'.

It would be reasonable to assume that the deep-water fish had regressed in the same way. However, far from being blind, they have the most sensitive eyes in the whole animal kingdom. Furthermore, the eyes are often very large and protruding: they can turn in almost any direction.

What exactly do they have eyes to see? It is the light that they themselves produce in special organs scattered over their bodies. Some of the mucous glands that open out onto the surface of the skin secrete a phosphorescent substance, and this can be seen as spots of light of various colours.

How is this light exploited?

Some quite rare fish even have an organ resembling a searchlight on their heads: as well as a small reservoir of luminous mucous it contains a jelly-like lens which is transparent and so increases the brightness of the light. These fish can therefore focus the light they produce onto the fish they hunt.

The luminous bait the angler-fish dangles before its victims is another example of fish producing light in order to survive.

A selection of deep-water fish. Bottom right: a hatchet-fish (Argyropelecus); Bottom left: a dragonfish; Top left: a pelican fish; Top right: a Chauliodus.

MARINE REPTILES

Are there crocodiles in the sea?

The sea crocodile drowns its prey before devouring it. But when it cannot find living victims, it eats carrion.

Crocodiles are usually found in the fresh water of rivers and swamps. Some species are quite at home in the brackish water of lagoons and river mouths. But the **sea crocodile from the Indian Ocean** and the South Pacific often goes a long way out to sea. It is voracious and extremely dangerous. It can be up to 20 feet (six m.) long. The female hatches out its eggs on the beach by sleeping all day on top of the hole in the sand where she laid them. At night she goes off to hunt for food.

Another, smaller crocodile can be found on the beaches of the West Atlantic from Florida down to the north of South America. This too is a very dangerous creature to encounter.

What do turtles feed on?

If you have ever had a tortoise you must have fed it on lettuce leaves and the like. But they also like more substantial food, such as slugs and snails, and are therefore of great assistance to gardeners.

Turtles are also both vegetarian and carnivorous. Their normal diet consists of seaweed, crustacea, molluscs and fish, and is healthy enough for them to reach an appreciable size.

The green turtle that inhabits warm waters—including the Mediterranean —can weigh up to **one thousand pounds** (four hundred and fifty kilograms). It is used for making great quantities of turtle soup.

Turtles do not have teeth, but their jaws are covered with a horny substance that has a sharp cutting edge. This horny substance therefore serves as the turtle's teeth.

Why do turtles lay their eggs on the beach?

Turtles and tortoises are reptiles. Like all reptiles—snakes, lizards and crocodiles—they lay eggs. The eggs need warmth to hatch out. When it is time to lay their eggs, turtles come out of the sea, dragging themselves along on their **legs.** These legs have taken on the **form of fins** and are no longer adapted to walking. They dig big holes in the sand and lay about a thousand eggs each in them. They then fill in the hole very carefully, smoothing out the surface so as to prevent the nest from being discovered. The sun, by heating the sand, hatches out the eggs: after six or seven weeks **hundreds of baby turtles** come out of the holes. As fast as their legs will drag them they head for the sea to escape the birds who have been waiting for them to hatch out.

The leathery turtle lays between sixty and one hundred and fifty eggs a year. They hatch out after a period of two months.

Does every turtle have a shell?

The leathery turtle.

A turtle's **shell** is like a box of bone covered with horn: down the back it is welded to the spinal column. But there are some turtles who do not have the bony covering. These kinds of turtle have just tiny flat bones sunk into their thick, leathery skin which is covered with horny plates. The leathery turtle—the biggest of the turtles—does not have a shell. It can weigh anything up to 1,300 pounds (600 kg.) and is probably the heaviest living reptile.

It is quite a rare animal, although it lives in the tropical regions of all the oceans.

Where does 'tortoise shell' come from?

A tortoise can provide about four to six pounds of tortoise-shell. The lighter shades are the most expensive.

Tortoise-shell comes from a **tropical species of turtle.** The horny plates covering its shell overlap like tiles on a roof. Like all reptiles, turtles love to bask in the sun. When they come up to the surface to sun themselves they can be caught quite easily. One turtle provides between **four and six pounds of tortoise-shell,** the lighter shades being the most sought after.

MARINE MAMMALS

How deep can a whale dive?

The whale is a huge mass of flesh and fat. Its blubber is very thick—about eighteen inches—and gives it good protection against knocks and water pressure. This enables it to go deep under the water without feeling any ill effects. It can dive quickly to a depth of about **5,000 feet** (1,500 m.). At this depth every square inch of its body is subject to a pressure of about **1,000 pounds** (450 kg.).

The whale's lungs can hold vast quantities of air enabling the animal to stay underwater for between 30 to 50 minutes. As the whale comes back up to the surface its spout sprays water several yards into the air. It blows a dozen or so times before going down again.

A comb in the mouth of some whales filters plankton. Sperm whales do not have this bony comb.

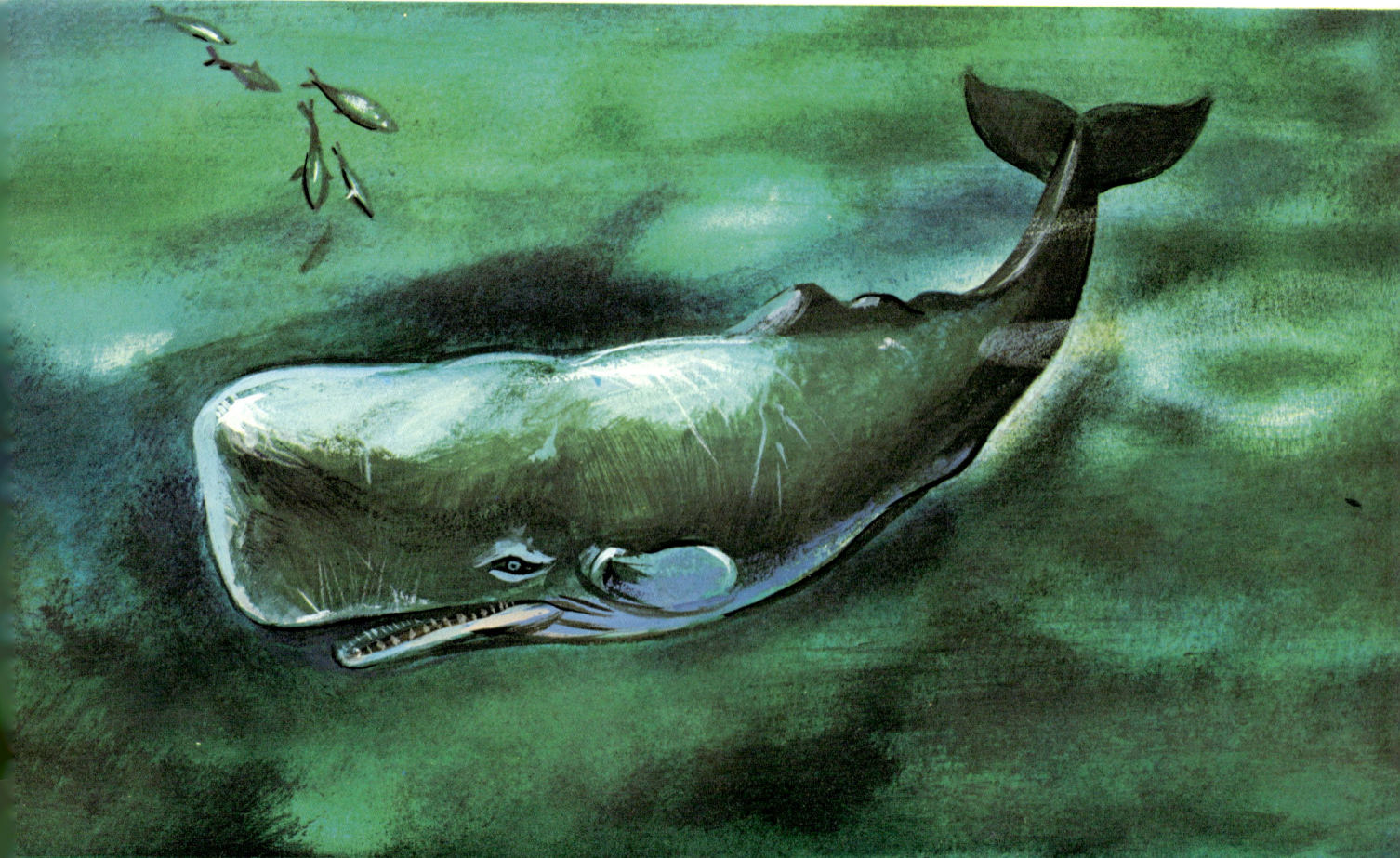

Why do stranded whales die?

Although **whales breathe air,** they suffocate when they are stranded on a beach.

The whale is a huge animal. The **blue whale** is probably the biggest animal that has ever lived. Its mass of flesh and blubber is supported only by a weak skeleton. Its great bulk presents no problems when it is surrounded by water. Its enormous size works in its favour when it is in the water, because it provides a proportionately large buoyancy force. But when this support is missing its internal organs are crushed by the weight of its flesh and fat. A stranded whale can **fill its lungs** only at the expense of great muscular effort. It rapidly runs out of breath and the heart soon tires as it pumps blood into organs now flattened by the weight. It is unable to move on land, and dies **crushed under its own weight.**

Can dolphins talk?

These sea animals have aroused a great deal of interest in recent years, and things are said about them that are not quite true.

Some people, for example, say that they can pronounce words! Advanced research has been done on the way dolphins communicate with each other, but they in fact have no vocal cords. On the other hand, **they can whistle** by blowing air through their blowholes. So one scientist had the idea of teaching them a 'whistle language' rather like the one used by some shepherds in the mountains when they are a long way off from one another. It takes rather a long time, but the dolphins are eventually able to respond to such a language.

A dolphin jumps to catch the fish held out by its trainer. The tail movement that enables it to reach this height can be clearly seen.

Dolphins are cheerful animals. They love to play and readily do the tricks they have been taught. But the one thing they do not like is injections! When they are ill they do everything possible to avoid being 'jabbed'.

How is a baby dolphin born?

Baby dolphins behave very affectionately towards their mothers. They rub themselves against them, making contented little noises. It is thought that dolphins can reproduce from the age of about seven, but generally speaking the parents in 'schools' of dolphins are rather older. Their exact life-span is not known, but in one American marineland there is a dolphin over thirty years old and still in excellent shape.

The **dolphin is a mammal** like a dog, a cat or a monkey. Any resemblance it may have to a fish ends with its outside appearance. When it comes to the surface it breathes in air with its lungs. A baby dolphin grows inside its mother for a period of eleven or twelve months. A great fuss is made when it is due to be born. The other female dolphins surround the mother, and the males station themselves at points along this circle in order to ward off attackers. It would indeed be an unlucky shark who came along at that moment, since a **blow** from a dolphin's jaw could easily knock it out or even kill it.

The baby dolphin comes out of its mother tail first and not head first like most other mammals. It takes between half an hour and an hour for it to come right out. As soon as it does come out two females take it to the surface on their fins: they duck it under the water two or three times, and this makes it squeal and so fill its lungs with air. This is just like smacking the bottom of a new-born baby.

But unlike a human baby, the baby dolphin is already more capable of looking after itself, and a few minutes after being born is able to swim alongside its mother. From time to time it is fed with very dense, fatty **milk.** It stays very close to its mother for about 18 months, and is quickly gathered in by a fin if it wanders off too far.

How can dolphins navigate without using their eyes?

There are certain types of whistle that a dog hears, but which are completely inaudible to a man. These whistles send out **ultrasonic waves** that do not make our eardrums vibrate. The dog is not the only animal to be able to pick up these sounds. The dolphin too has this capacity, and uses it mainly for making its way through murky waters. It can locate obstacles by sending out ultrasonic sounds which **rebound** and come straight back to it. It is more accurate to liken this to a sonar rather than to a radar system. A radar sends out radio waves, while a sonar sends out ultrasonic ones. Echolocation, as it is called, is used by fishermen to locate shoals of fish.

The dolphin has its own highly sensitive ultrasonic detector. One experiment was carried out by cutting a tennis ball in two and placing one half over each **eye.** The dolphin was then put into a pool full of streamers floating downwards from tiny bells. Thanks to its **natural sonar,** the dolphin was able to negotiate the obstacles without ringing the bells. The blind species found in the muddy waters of the Ganges navigate and find their food perfectly well by using this system. It is thought that their eyes declined because they were useless in such murky waters.

How is the dolphin able to swim so fast?

The shape of a dolphin's body is perfectly adapted for moving rapidly through the water, but this alone does not explain why it can reach speeds of up to 38 miles an hour (60 kph.).

It has been endowed with a remarkable skin. It is very smooth and completely bald, thus offering no resistance to the water which flows unhindered over it. Tiny marine animals could anchor themselves to it, but the dolphin **peels** regularly and its skin remains clean and smooth. The skin is very soft to the touch; the blubber beneath it encloses a muscular layer that gives the dolphin an amazing degree of **manoeuvrability.** The blubber helps it to heal very quickly if its skin is torn.

The dolphin's muscles are especially strong in its tail. You only have to see one **stand up** and 'walk' in the water to have proof of that.

How can a seal stay so long underwater?

When a man holds his breath his sight becomes blurred very rapidly, and he can even fall unconscious due to the brain's lack of oxygen. The seal is an excellent swimmer and can stay underwater for between **20 and 30 minutes.** How can it go so long without breathing?

Its lungs can stretch to take in very large amounts of air. Along certain blood vessels there are **small reservoirs** where oxygen is **stored.** In addition, the blood circulation can be stopped in certain parts of the body so as to keep up the supply of blood—and hence of oxygen—to the vital part, the seal's brain.

A young seal.